My Heart's Desire

A Journey Toward Finding Extravagant Love

MARY SINGER WICK

Outskirts Press, Inc.
Denver, Colorado

Outskirts Press, Inc.
http://www.outskirtspress.com

ISBN: 978-1-60725-152-1

Library of Congress Control Number: 2008942968

Outskirts Press and the "OP" logo are trademarks belonging to Outskirts Press, Inc.

PRINTED IN THE UNITED STATES OF AMERICA

What People Are Saying About *My Heart's Desire: A Journey Toward Finding Extravagant Love*

"What a compelling, and heartfelt book! Mary Singer Wick offers a poignant and honest portrayal of her myriad experiences, and how she eventually comes to find herself through a direct relationship with God. For anyone who doubts the presence of a higher power, this book will give your heart wings and make you want to sing from the top of a mountain! Mary is an incredibly talented writer to burst on the scene, and her style is both polished and profound. I couldn't put the book down! *My Heart's Desire* can be compared to a five-star restaurant—each chapter a most delicious course that eventually leaves you feeling both full and satisfied. Five stars to *My Heart's Desire*. I would recommend this book to anyone looking for the next *Purpose Driven Life*. It's that good!"

- Sally Shields bestselling author of
The Daughter-in-Law Rules: 101 Surefire Ways to Manage (and Make Friends with) Your Mother-in-Law!
www.theDILRules.com

"No matter how long you have waited for your true love you will enjoy discovering the love of a lifetime in *My Heart's Desire*."

- Deanna Falchook author of *To Be A Mother*

"Honest, intimate, absorbing and true. Mary Singer Wick assesses her *real* life and her *real* needs with powerful clarity illuminated by great hope. What an encouraging read for both the seeker and the believer."

– Allison Snyder, Women's Ministry, Providence Baptist Church, Raleigh, North Carolina

"I was immediately drawn into the story and felt her emotions as she walked from the shadows into the wonderful light. What an inspiring journey! You will be glad you read it."

- Edith Jackson author of *Broken Bread and Poured Out Wine, Spiritual Food for Hungry Pilgrims*

"This book is simply delightful. It's an easy read that will capture your heart and make it soar to believe God's promises."

- Elaine M. Epps, Atlanta, GA

"God knows and hears our heart-cries. Mary shares hope and fulfillment, from loneliness to her "Heart's Desire." Compelling and encouraging, with a challenge to turn our own hearts towards obedience and trust in God's plans."

– Catherine Sullivan, Woman to Woman Mentoring, Providence Baptist Church, Raleigh, North Carolina

"Mary's way with words is relatable while touching a spot deep in your heart. I found myself in many of her pages and walked away with a new sense of how much our Savior loves us."

- Sarah Jane entrepreneur, New Hampshire

Contents

Acknowledgements
and Disclaimer

I would like to thank my family and friends who persevered with me in prayer not only while I wrote this book, but throughout the many seasons of my life.

To everyone who walked beside me on those stormy rain-filled days, and danced with me on warm sunny afternoons, I thank God for you! Your love and support has been one of life's greatest treasures.

A special thank you to the many dedicated women who gave up their precious time to proofread *My Heart's Desire: A Journey Toward Finding Extravagant Love*. I couldn't have accomplished this without you!

To my husband, Jon, who listened patiently and believed in my calling. Thank you for your love and encouragement! I'm so very happy to be your wife.

This book chronicles seven years of my life, and is composed of personal experiences that were written to the best of my recollection, and subject to my interpretation. All individuals referenced in this story, outside of God, Jon and me, were not mentioned by name. In some cases, brief descriptions were included to show a person's significance in my life without jeopardizing their confidentiality. This was done to protect their privacy, and to respect their personal viewpoints which may differ from my own.

All glory, praise, and thanksgiving to Almighty God who is the Author of my life, and the reason this story is told.

Mary Singer Wick

Introduction

Have you ever made a promise you really didn't think you'd have to keep? You know--something you say in passing that you'll do someday, but you're not exactly making a sincere commitment to do it. You don't really believe it will ever be brought up in conversation again, and you've forgotten yourself that you even said it. But what if that person you made a promise to was God and not only did He not forget what you said, but He wouldn't let you forget it either.

In the summer of 1997, shortly before turning 39, my struggle with singleness reached new heights. I'd been engaged before, but never married. With the ominous big "4-0" looming in my future, I wondered if true love would forever remain an elusive dream. Often a topic of intense discussion among close girlfriends; we'd analyze every new relationship hoping to make this one work out. For many of my friends it didn't seem to be as difficult; they married relatively young. But for those of us in the over-thirty-five group the statistics were grim; encouragement was scarcely found.

Searching for evidence to silence the critics claiming my prime had passed, I began reading love stories of other people's triumphs. Unfortunately, the books I read in 1997 failed to inspire me. Instead, their stories frustrated me because the people sharing them were in their twenties.

They hadn't experienced two decades of the singles scene like I had. Many married their first or second boyfriend or girlfriend. As I read their reflections on loneliness, and all they had suffered in their struggle to find love, I closed the book loudly proclaiming, "You have no idea!"

That's when, flippantly, I promised God if He ever blessed me with a good husband, and a happy marriage, I'd write our story offering middle-aged singles hope. This promise was never shared. On the contrary, it was quietly buried below my consciousness until recent years when God resurfaced it.

My first response was to dismiss its significance, and question my own sanity! But the Lord would not let me off the hook so easily. While praying for confirmation, He ignited my passion to share this love story; refusing to give me rest.

So here I am in 2008, approaching my sixth wedding anniversary, as I place before you my journey from single-hood to married life. This story is so much more than that. It's a tale of first falling in love with Jesus, and becoming His bride, before I met my future husband, Jon. As you read this book, I pray you will find hope and encouragement as you travel the paths the Lord took me on that led me to my heart's desire.

Blessings,
Mary Singer Wick

Chapter 1
From North to South

"Delight yourself in the Lord and He will give you the
desires of your heart" (Psalm 37:4 NIV).

As summers go, 1997 was one of my better ones. I
was finally beginning to enjoy life again after three
years of dire circumstances, most of which I'd kept hidden
from the outside world with the exception of a few close
friends. I'd spent 11 years in Boston, Massachusetts after
leaving my family behind in Syracuse, New York to pursue
an adventurous life in a big city. I worked hard to establish
myself there, but by 1994 things were rapidly beginning to
unravel. I was suffering the consequences of wrong choices
I'd made over the years and was beginning to examine how
I was spending my time on earth. As I reflected on those
floundering years, I admitted I had wasted and misused
much of what God had given me, and it was time for a
change.

...me had come for me to close down a failed business ...re I'd begun four years earlier, and to end a tumultuous five-year relationship with a man with whom I was hopelessly in love. Our relationship was unhealthy from the start. I'd compromised on some of my deepest values by getting involved with him, but his charming good looks and risk-taker personality were hard to resist. Over time, our lives became so entangled physically and emotionally that I couldn't easily break away. This wasn't the first time I found myself in a relationship where I'd sacrificed more of my heart and soul for a man than he was willing to give, but it was definitely the longest and most costly affair to not only to my pocketbook, but also my self esteem.

He promised we'd have a future together, and that I'd be able to quit my full-time job as an administrative assistant once my business was profitable and his career was stable. But there never seemed to be enough money to meet our expenses, and with marriage contingent upon our financial success, I felt like I was forever chasing an unattainable carrot dangling in front of me. In all fairness, I was no innocent victim. I'd made it much too convenient for him to use money as an excuse not to marry me, and over the years we both lost respect for each other. In the end, I'd grown weary of trying to make our plans come to fruition. The mental torture this "arrangement" was putting me through was eroding my hope. Our love affair had cost me dearly. In the five years we'd been together, I'd expended almost all my energy and money on building this dream of self employment and was now $30,000 in credit card debt.

This debt was like an open wound draining the life out of me as lender fees from missed payments and bounced checks mounted. I had to stop the bleeding. Each day seemed harder than the previous one as I mourned the loss of my future with this man, and my good credit rating. I was barely able to sleep; stress and grief were my constant unwelcome companions. My life was a mess financially and emotionally, and I was ashamed I'd let it get so out of control. Some days it was hard to get out of bed, and I worried I might be slipping into a state of depression. I couldn't stand living like this anymore. It was time to take action and find a way to break the relentless cycle of pain. Eventually, I found the courage to cut off all contact with my long-time lover, and to close down my failed business permanently. But there was still more to be done.

My credit card debt exceeded my annual salary as an administrative assistant, and I had no way to pay it off unless I found work in a higher-paying field. Several people advised me to file for bankruptcy, but I declined. This debt was a result of my own bad decisions and I wanted to repay all that I owed. By 1995, the job market and hiring needs had slowed in Boston; the same was true for Syracuse; so I investigated moving to another part of the country. Raleigh, North Carolina was touted as one of the top cities in the U.S. to live and to work in, and I had an ally there--a cherished college friend and her husband. When I contacted her, she enthusiastically offered to help me in my transition, so I made arrangements to stay with them. Over the next three months I traveled back and forth from Boston to Raleigh for job interviews.

Persistence paid off, and, by September, I accepted a job offer for a technical recruiting position with a national staffing agency in Raleigh. It was exactly the opportunity I'd been hoping for! For the first time in my life, I would receive a base salary with the potential to earn a commission. The cost of living was much lower in Raleigh than Boston, and if I controlled my spending I'd pay off this seemingly insurmountable debt one day. As I loaded my tiny frame into a 25-foot rental truck and set off on that solitary 14-hour drive, I envisioned the move as a chance to reinvent myself in a city where I had total anonymity. Suffering was the catalyst that propelled me to start anew, and as I waved goodbye to the hardships of Boston, I eagerly anticipated saying hello to boom times in Raleigh. I was grateful to be leaving the aggressive environment of the northeast, and was looking forward to settling into a gentler pace in a southern climate.

Although tired and lonely when I left New England, my heart clung to the hope that somewhere in Raleigh I'd one day find the love and happiness I was seeking. Even after all the heartbreak I'd endured, I managed to get back in touch with my optimistic spirit. That's not unusual for a woman like me whose favorite childhood movie was "The Sound of Music". And like the main character Maria, always believed everything would turn out alright if I had enough "confidence in me".

While in many ways Raleigh was everything Boston wasn't, I still led a fast-paced life when it came to my job. Technical recruiting was a highly stressful and competitive industry and required my utmost focus in order to be successful. Although I'd moved to a much smaller city with less amenities and a more people-friendly environment, it required a lot of effort on my part getting started in a new career, familiarizing myself with my surroundings, and trying to meet socially compatible people. Initially, the only people I knew were my college friend and her husband who were busy raising two young sons, so I had to expand my circle of friends. This didn't happen overnight. In fact, it took me almost a year to meet other single people with whom I shared common interests.

One of the greatest breakthroughs I received for making new acquaintances was a recommendation from a co-worker that I join the local ski and outing club. I heeded her advice and attended one of their member meetings in February, 1996. I have to admit, it was a little intimidating walking solo into a room full of 400 people, even for an extrovert like me. But when I glanced around the room at all the happy faces, my fears were transformed into excitement and I thought, *"This must be the place to be!"* I joined the club that night and promptly began attending a variety of activities. While I didn't make new friends right away I had hope that I would soon. Each time I went to an outing I had a mission in mind. I'd toss a few of my business cards into my backpack, and if I met someone interesting I'd give them one suggesting we organize a coed get together. To my surprise and delight, everyone I gave my business card to called! Although it was never broadcasted, I suspected they may have been just as lonely as I was and wanted to have something to do on the weekends, too.

Like me, many were part of the great migration to Raleigh seeking a new start, a better life, and perhaps healing from their own wounds and hardships. We seemed to share a common pioneer spirit having left our comfort zone to seek good fortune in a new land. The Raleigh natives eagerly embraced us, and our group was brimming with an over abundance of positive energy. By the summer of 1996, I was quickly becoming the pied piper of invitations to group outings. I couldn't tolerate the thought of a nice person being alone, so I continued to invite new people into our ever-expanding circle of friends. Most of the time, it was I who was leading the way and controlling the social agenda. This made me feel important and needed by the group. It was the first time in my life that I was revered as a leader among my peers. I was overjoyed every time I thought about how much better my life was now compared to what it had been only a year earlier.

That summer was the start of the most fun I'd had since college only this was even better. I had money at my disposal! We were all single working professionals in our twenties and thirties with the same goal in mind—work hard and make new friends! There was always something to do, and even the simplest activities such as making dinner or taking a walk together at a local park became a treasured moment. I was dating different men and enjoying the experience even though no serious attachments had been formed. My work was equally satisfying to me. Each month my commission check was steadily increasing, and I was making great strides in paying down my credit card debt. Even though I still owed over $25,000, I was exceedingly proud of the progress I had made. Each day was a continuous flurry of activity, and I no longer had time to grieve over my painful past. While my new life was full of good things, something wasn't quite right.

By 1997, I was feeling on top of the world and totally indestructible. At last, I finally had my life in order and had assumed personal responsibility for forming our group of friends. I never thought to give credit to the One who deserved all the glory--God. I was too busy thinking it was I who was holding everything in place. If someone in our circle had a problem, it was I who tried to fix it. While I did care about helping my friends, sometimes I cared much more about the pride I felt inside myself for coming up with the solution they needed. As the circle widened, I vowed to keep up with everyone's needs both socially and emotionally as much as I could. They were wonderful friends to me, but up until this point I hadn't needed their support as much as I needed to give them mine in order to bolster my self esteem.

Inside I'd begun feeling very tired again; afraid this circle of friends was going to disband if I didn't keep us united. I was scared I would soon have to step down from my self-proclaimed throne and relinquish my scepter to someone else. *What would my friends think if they saw me weak and vulnerable?* I didn't want to be wide-open emotionally with anyone. It was much easier to be happy and polite; focusing on their concerns while never revealing my own. I was right. A change had been set in motion, and I would be stepping aside, but the successor was not who I thought it would be.

Chapter 2
The Beginning of Change

"I am the vine; you are the branches. If a man remains in me and I in him, he will bear much fruit; apart from me you can do nothing" (John 15:5 NIV).

I n the spring of 1997, I'd begun to notice some changes in my body. My stomach was a little swollen, and I was going to the bathroom more frequently. At first I attributed this to all the water I consumed as part of my healthy lifestyle. As a former aerobics instructor, daily workouts had long been a passion of mine not only to look good, but to eliminate stress. I didn't smoke, rarely drank, and ate very healthy meals with some occasional binges. I took an active interest in my health and diligently studied the latest nutritional trends. At 39-years-old, my heart still harbored a hope for marriage and children; I strived to be in excellent shape to ensure my offspring would be healthy too. Never did I want to hear a doctor say, "If you had taken better care of yourself this problem wouldn't be happening now."

My weight tends to settle in my hips, but my stomach has always been flat no matter what I weighed. In fact, my flat stomach and small waist was one of the physical features people commented on the most. I was wearing petite sizes two and four, so it didn't make sense that my stomach wasn't flat anymore. It wasn't anything other people noticed, but I did. One day, while showering, I saw a bulge about the size of a quarter on the left side of my abdomen, and it startled me. My first reaction was to cry, even though I wasn't in any pain. I touched the bulge and pressed it into my intestinal area where it disappeared from sight. I had no idea what it was but knew it shouldn't be ignored. Immediately I sought medical advice.

Recent changes to our employee healthcare plan forced me to find a new doctor. Scouring the pages of the directory, I noticed a female internist close to work. Upon talking to her cordial office assistant, I learned she was accepting new patients and could see me right away. The day of my appointment, I sat nervously waiting to be called when the doctor was ready. Suddenly, I spotted a brochure about uterine fibroids and began reading the pamphlet. *"What were fibroids?"* I wondered. No one had ever mentioned them to me, so I was ignorant about the subject.

Glancing through the brochure, fear washed over me after reading that while these tumors are rarely cancerous, they can cause infertility. Quickly and discretely I placed the folded pamphlet on the table saying to myself, *"Stop! Don't let thoughts about fibroids enter into your mind!"* In my warped belief, I thought if I didn't embrace any knowledge regarding infertility then it couldn't adversely affect my ability to conceive. The idea of never having a baby was such an emotionally-charged topic for me; one I wasn't willing to entertain. Nothing could be more disturbing than to be told I was barren. Silently, I prayed in that waiting room that whatever this bulge was it wasn't the dreaded word—a fibroid.

Relief was swift when the doctor examined me and said, "Oh, you don't have fibroids. It's just a muscle. You're in too good of shape to have fibroids." *Hallelujah! Now I can breathe.* She proceeded to tell me the bulge was a hernia, and recommended a specialist I should contact. That diagnosis caught me off guard. I couldn't imagine how I'd developed a hernia. My brothers had them as infants, but no women in my family did. Although I was a little worried about what would be my first surgery, at least I didn't have fibroids.

In July, I met with the specialist. After examining me, we agreed the date for my hernia surgery would be in mid-September since I wasn't in immediate danger. I needed time to realign my workload, and to make arrangements for my mother to arrive from Syracuse to care for me. Over the next two months, I continued my healthy routine of exercising and eating well as I prepared for surgery. Because I was giving my body the attention it needed, I was confident I'd have a smooth and quick recovery. No longer was I concerned about fibroids. I assumed the hernia was responsible for my protruding abdomen and frequent bathroom visits. Once the surgery was behind me I'd be back to tip-top shape, at least that's what I thought.

My mother arrived the eve of my surgery; quickly settling

in. Early next morning, we entered the hospital where after a few minutes of prepping I was whisked into surgery. Having never been in an operating room before the coldness surprised me. Everyone was wearing turtlenecks under their hospital coats. As my arms were out-stretched like a "T" and an I.V. line was inserted, a wave of fear rolled over me. *I'm about to be cut open!* Noticing my shaky legs, the observant staff made pleasant remarks to ease my nervousness. I liked the team and felt I was in good hands.

When the doctor walked in and looked at my abdomen he said, "Why didn't someone tell me she's pregnant? I just saw her a few weeks ago and she didn't have an ounce of fat on her." I told him it was impossible for me to be pregnant barring another miracle conception because I wasn't having sex. The last thing I remember the doctor saying to me was, "I want to talk with you about this next week when you come in for your post-operative exam." That didn't sound too good to me, but I had no time to respond. He told me to count backwards from 10 and within seconds I was unconscious.

The next thing I knew, I was in the recovery room where nurses were talking to me. Turns out I didn't have a hernia. Instead, I had a hydrocele which is a saclike cavity containing an accumulation of fluid. The doctor had drained and sealed it off, and said I should recover just fine. I was released that afternoon and spent the rest of the day recuperating in my apartment with my mother and friends by my side. This was my mother's first trip to Raleigh, and nice for her to meet the good people she'd heard so much about from me. Back home, my family was relieved I'd made it through surgery with no complications.

A week later, Mom took me to my post-operative visit before flying home. With no sign of infection the doctor declared me fit to work. Scribbling on a notepad, he casually tossed out words as destructive to me as dynamite, "Since you're not pregnant you must have a very large fibroid. I don't do hysterectomies; you'll have to see an OB/GYN about that. You'll feel much better afterwards." *What does he mean I'll feel better? How could destroying something so precious bring comfort? Why such a drastic measure? Is there no happy medium? My symptoms are so mild; there must be some mistake.* Sensing my disbelief, his nurse studied my face; her eyes mirroring my own with an expression of total shock.

Granted an epiphany, the doctor realized he'd startled me and began back-peddling in a feeble attempt to ease my horror. He wasn't sure if I needed a hysterectomy, only an OB/GYN could determination that. *How can he be so trivial in his response; acting as if my uterus can be so easily discarded?* There I was fresh from surgery, still feeling the pain, and he's recommending another abdominal surgery; the most unimaginable one possible! Emerging from his office, I never breathed a word of this news to my mother. It seemed unfair to burden her now as she readied to board a plane. All I shared was that I was cleared to return to work. Later that night I broke my silence to my roommate. She burst into tears saying, "How can you go through another surgery when you just had one?" Joining her in her tears, I agreed this had escalated much too quickly. There must be better options available than a hysterectomy.

My first phone call was to my friend who'd help me relocate to Raleigh. She and her husband were expecting twin boys in October. I knew she'd know a trusted gynecologist

I could see for advice. She suggested her doctor who she believed was accepting new patients. When I called his office, he ordered an ultrasound for me on October 1st before we met. He wanted the results prior to my appointment so we could review them together. My girlfriend offered to meet me at the hospital; I gladly accepted.

Although the technician was professional and friendly, she wouldn't let me see the screen thus adding to the mystery, and my anxiety, over this situation. She said I had several fibroids; one in particular was large. My friend did her best to speak words of comfort, but her face couldn't hide her distress. As I lay on the examination table, with a gel-covered wand being rubbed across my protruding belly, I was caught up in the irony of the moment. Here was my friend, pregnant with twins, carrying her two-year-old son on her hip while my hope for having children is fading with each health update. *"This can't be happening to me"*, was all I could think.

Now it was no longer an imaginary fear I could ignore, but a reality I had to face. I had uterine fibroids and needed to educate myself on what my options were. Hearing the technician confirm this truth had turned my world upside down. Night and day it was all I could think about, but I stretched myself to remain optimistic. I couldn't surrender so easily. Perhaps when I met with the doctor he'd offer better and less invasive solutions than a hysterectomy. With a doctor appointment on the horizon, it was time to share the news with my family, and a few close friends, who could offer support. Right now, it wasn't the kind of thing I was willing to reveal to a lot of people, especially my guy friends. Oddly enough, I felt telling people about this latest health challenge would be more of a let-down to them than it was to me. They'd all been so supportive during my hernia surgery last month, how could I ask for more of their attention so soon? I longed to be back in control of my life; be a caregiver again, not the care-receiver I was now.

My appointment with the gynecologist was in late October which afforded me a few weeks to regroup emotionally, and continue healing physically from my current surgery. I tried very hard not to get too upset, but inside I battled discouragement, as I wondered why God was putting me through this. Up until now, everything seemed to be going so well for me these past two years. All of a sudden my life was slipping backwards again, and I felt powerless to stop it. *Where was He leading me this time?* Wherever it was, it didn't feel good, and I didn't think I had the strength for another setback in my life.

Chapter 3
Searching for a Cure

"It is better to trust in the Lord than to put confidence in man" (Psalm 118:8 NIV).

The day arrived for my gynecologist appointment; I went into his office armed with my questions and concerns. Immediately his quirky sense of humor and kind demeanor put me at ease. He made me laugh (not something I recall doing before with an OB/GYN) which diminished much of my tension. His exam revealed my uterus was swollen to the size of a 12-week pregnancy. The ultrasound captured several fibroids within its view, but they were too numerous to count accurately. The largest was approximately the size of an orange; it was situated on top of my bladder. When I imagined holding an orange in my palm I got a sense of how big that fibroid was, and found it hard to believe there were others inside me.

Unfortunately, the doctor said fibroids were not easily cured. There was medication that if consumed would force my body into a menopausal state resulting in less estrogen production, which was believed to encourage fibroid growth. But this was, at best, a temporary solution. I could only take the medication for a few months in an attempt to shrink the fibroids prior to surgically removing them. The doctor said it would be a tough route to go, but one worth considering. Even if I had the fibroids removed there was no guarantee they wouldn't grow back again. In his opinion, I had two options available. The first was a myomectomy to remove the fibroid tumors without taking my uterus. It's a very delicate surgery accompanied by the risk of bleeding out; resulting in an emergency hysterectomy. My fibroids were located within the uterine wall as well as inside the cavity. This would make my surgery even more challenging for a surgeon. The second choice was a hysterectomy to which I strongly objected. He listened compassionately and said he understood.

As we explored the myomectomy option further, the doctor explained most woman wait to have this surgery right before they want to conceive. *"Well, that's not my situation,"* I thought. I didn't know when I'd attempt to have a baby, but I knew I wouldn't do it while single. Since I wasn't in any eminent danger, he agreed I had time to mull things over. Sympathetically, he apologized for not being able to give me, a 39-year-old unmarried woman, much of a guarantee I'd have a baby one day. How sad to hear those words.

I rose up to leave, as the appointment concluded, when a plaque on his wall caught my attention. Without hesitation I fixed on its words and did my best to memorize them,

"Those who hope in the Lord will renew their
They will soar like eagles; they will run and not grow
weary. They will walk and not be faint" (Isaiah 40:31
NIV). Being unfamiliar with a lot of Scriptures, and this
one was no exception; I somehow sensed God was sending
a message of confirmation to resist making any decisions
about surgery. At that moment, another option came to me;
one that deserved worthy consideration. Turning to the doctor, before I exited the room, I asked if I could investigate a
choice he hadn't presented. I wanted to conduct research on
holistic ways of healing myself. He agreed by saying that
because I was in otherwise exceptional health I would
make a good "science experiment". Perhaps I'd be the
woman to introduce him, and the medical community, to
new methods that were more natural ways to shrink fibroids. If I was successful, he promised he'd share this information with other woman seeking alternative ways of
healing themselves. We'd evaluate my findings at my next
appointment in January, 1998.

As I left his office, and drove back to work, I didn't feel
any better. It wasn't his fault he couldn't supply me with a
less invasive solution to my problem, but that didn't soothe
my disappointment. In successfully bargaining to buy myself more time, I'd transferred the pressure onto me to find
my own cure. If I failed I would need surgery. With no serious boyfriend in my life the decision was mine alone to
make. Given the choice between a myomectomy and a hysterectomy I'd definitely chose the myomectomy. But I
wasn't ready to take the gamble that I could wake up from
surgery having to be told I had a hysterectomy due to complications. Nor was I willing to risk that after a successful
myomectomy the fibroids could reappear in the future.
Deep inside I believed there had to be other choices for me

that I just hadn't discovered yet.

Just be strong Mary; don't panic. At least you don't have cancer; things could be much worse. Miracles happen all the time; maybe you'll be one of those who experiences one. These were some of the things I told myself to resurrect my optimistic spirit. After all, the fibroids could magically disappear, or I could meet the man of my dreams who'd be supportive no matter what the outcome was. Anything is possible. I had to keep my hope alive. If I didn't not only would I give up the fight for a resolution, but I would scare any potential suitors away with my look of desperation. This was no time to panic. If I remained calm I'd be less prone to making a decision now I might regret later. New treatments might be on the horizon; I just needed to seek out who was involved in this discovery. My search for a cure was about to begin, but inside of me a much deeper search had already begun, even though I was yet to realize it.

Chapter 4
The Anger Within

… "for they loved the praise from men more than praise from God" (John 12:43 NIV).

In my exploration to unearth natural ways of purging these fibroids, and their toxic affect on me, I invited a close friend whose holistic expertise I admired to join me in my quest. We'd been former co-workers in Boston. While my path to establish a new life and career led me to North Carolina, she ventured to New Mexico. Witnessing her past success in treating various aliments, I trusted her counsel. Speaking on the phone, we formed a cooperative plan; promising to share our findings soon. *How fortunate I was to have this valuable confidant sharing in my investigation.*

As I scanned different articles one theme arose over and over—no one really knew what caused fibroids. They seemed to be connected to overproduction of estrogen, or general hormone imbalances, which led me to jokingly tell people, "I guess I'm too much of a woman!" Some of the literature said they were caused by poor diet; one that was high in fat and red meat, while low in fruits and vegetables. If a woman was sedentary and overweight she was more likely to get fibroids. Neither of those profiles described me or my lifestyle. Other authors suggested fibroids were related to emotional stress; women who stored sadness or anger in their core (also known as the abdominal or reproductive area) were prone to fibroids. Having been through some pretty traumatic events in the past five years, I thought perhaps my fibroids were a result of stress and unreleased emotions. This was a theory I could relate to.

While identifying a potential cause surfaced rather effortlessly, curing fibroids presented many conflicting options. All holistic practitioners agreed dietary changes accompanied by vitamins, herbs, meditation, and exercise were required, but differed on which combination thereof. The diets were outrageously strict suggesting many items be avoided until menopause, years away for me. The avoidance list included: dairy products, red meat, sugar, white and wheat flour, alcohol, chocolate (how cruel!) and caffeine. Non-organic eggs, poultry, fish, vegetables and fruits were banned as pesticides and growth hormones, often found in conventional foods, were deemed poisonous to me. Some restricted salt, pepper and soy products, others sanctioned them. One said eat only raw foods—nothing microwaveable. Several recommended various tea concoctions claiming they'd regulate my estrogen imbalance. Household cleaning products, considered dangerous culprits, had to be replaced with organic counterparts. Life's simple pleasures vanished as I found myself trapped in this mental prison of "do this but don't do that"; frantically planning my escape. It was maddening!

When I spoke with my friend in New Mexico, and compared what I'd learned with her research, I was able to nar-
row it down a little knowing it would be impossible to
avoid everything on the list completely. I would start out
eliminating caffeine, dairy products, sugar and red meat.
I'd eat as much organic poultry, fish, fruits and vegetables
as I could find, and told her I'd keep her posted on my progress. She agreed with my approach and recommended
some herbs that might help with my hormone imbalance.
While this diet plan seemed like a huge sacrifice, it would
be worth it if the fibroids shrank or dissipated completely. I
convinced myself I could follow these guidelines for the
next three months and would measure the results with my
doctor in January. I wanted to impress him and the medical
community; so I was highly motivated.

Initially, I didn't want to tell a lot of people about my fibroids. But with such a restrictive diet to follow I had to tell
all my friends, even the guys. They would know something
wasn't quite right if I didn't speak up, and I also needed
some emotional support from the group. When I finally got
up the nerve to say something, everyone was concerned but
glad I told them. They believed if anyone could cure themselves holistically and avoid surgery it was me. To the outside world I still projected the image of exceptional health
coupled with a positive attitude. While that was very sweet
of my friends to have such confidence in me, deep inside I
felt anything but positive. So far I'd managed to hide the
truth from everyone but myself. The reality was I was angry over having to fight against the prospect of another surgery in the middle of recovering from the hydrocele
operation. The stress of calculating what I could and

couldn't eat was exhausting. I was totally consumed with my health, and dietary restrictions, and was not enjoying my life.

Many days it was hard to get my head around the concept that my inability to process negative emotions might have caused my fibroids. Being a sensitive person, and not afraid to cry, I thought I had released most of my negative emotions. Yes, I experienced occasional pain over some big disappointments in my life, but I wasn't thinking about them night and day anymore. For the most part, I'd moved on and was happy with my new life in Raleigh. *So, why was this happening now when everything was finally on an upturn for me?* If I was to blame for these fibroids growing than I had the power to reverse them. I just had to try hard enough and have enough faith in the holistic formula I was following.

Knowing my friends and family were cheering me on, I was anxious to cross the finish line displaying the coveted prize of peak health; celebrating my victory with the world. Frazzled by my recent fall from a position of leadership in the fitness community, to one who was teetering on the brink of failure, I had little time to wallow in self-pity. The quicker I implemented my self-prescribed healing program, the sooner I'd reap the benefits. I truly believed it was my turn to receive a miracle, and that the disappearance of my fibroids without a surgeon's knife was the only possible scenario.

Three months later, at my second ultrasound exam, I was encouraged by the news. The fibroids hadn't grown. In fact, the doctor thought my uterus was measuring a little smaller which could mean things were improving. He asked me about the vitamins, herbs and diet I was following and said they were all healthy choices. So he agreed to let me continue on my path of alternative medicine, even though he said he had some doubts that the diet would really make a difference either way. He still believed it was a hormone imbalance and avoiding chocolate (or any food) wouldn't change that, but I was determined to prove him wrong. My trips to the bathroom were still rather frequent but tolerable. Completely healed from my hydrocele surgery, I was able to do all normal activities without any problems. My next visit with him was six months away and would give me more time to heal myself without surgery or drugs. I was convinced if I had more faith in what I was doing the results would speak for themselves.

Now that I was feeling better I decided to look for a more challenging job in another area of technical recruiting. In a most unusual circumstance, God brought someone into my life that would ultimately lead me to my next recruiting position. While my roommate and I were attending a Super Bowl party we met a couple from Boston. Their flight home was delayed until Monday due to a blizzard in Boston. The woman was in Raleigh representing her company in search of hiring a recruiter for their Raleigh office. My roommate discretely told her I was looking for a job and suggested she talk to me.

After we spoke she said to me, "Do you believe in fate?" I told her I did and she replied, "So do I. I believe my flight was cancelled today because I was supposed to meet you and I'll be giving you a job offer soon." I didn't want to tell her I had my doubts about that since she worked for a small privately-owned company. I was looking for a large corporation similar to the one I recruited for now. However, I agreed to take her business card and call her during the week to schedule an appointment to talk further. I figured it couldn't hurt to explore the possibilities within her company.

A week later she returned to Raleigh; arranging a meeting between us. Reviewing her company's mission she explained they were in start-up mode; looking to expand their Raleigh office. Although the job would require working longer hours than I currently was, the income potential was far greater. *So much for not working for a small company!* Aware I was interviewing elsewhere, she presented me with a package that exceeded all others. Happily, I accepted her terms and began working in February, 1998. Immediately, I was flown to Boston headquarters for a week-long training; allowing me to reconnect with old friends. One close friend was particularly excited about my new position. She'd made the transition from human resources into contract recruiting years earlier, and felt this latest job would provide a much-needed distraction for me. I'd be too preoccupied learning my new role to be sulking about my health.

It was time to start over again and create a new image of myself to those around me. My plan was to be very successful in my work while keeping my distance from my co-workers. I didn't plan to spend time with them socially, but would be friendly and professional at work. Since there were only six of us in the Raleigh office I wanted them to know as little about my private life as possible. But that wasn't God's plan I would later learn.

Chapter 5
The Wrong Way

"There is a way that seems right to a man, but in the end it leads to death" (Proverbs 14:12 NIV).

O ur office staff of six quickly grew to 12 as business needs increased. Working through many a lunch hour, I often ate at my cubicle surrounded by curious eyes. My co-workers nicknamed me "stick chick" and often solicited my advice on healthy diet and nutritional choices. I hadn't divulged my fibroid secret or why I avoided dairy and caffeine. They just assumed I was lactose intolerant like another woman in the office. I felt guilty that I led them to believe I had the same problem with dairy she did. But since my health wasn't interfering with my work I didn't see the need to discuss it publicly. Besides, I believed if I stayed positive, and focused on the solution rather than the problem, my fibroids would shrink and there would be no reason to reveal my struggle.

Such was my attitude about my financial situation. While I'd reduced my debt from $30,000 to just over $20,000, I still wasn't able to consolidate any of it. However, by negotiating with the lenders, I managed to get the interest rates lowered a little on each credit card. Instead of worrying constantly about this large sum that I owed, I chose to focus my energy on working hard to increase my monthly commission. The more money I made the faster I could pay off the debt completely. Then I'd be happy! The more successful I was at work the better off my health would be too. I was convinced that I had the power within me to make right all the wrongs in my life, but I knew I couldn't do it alone anymore. So I began searching for others who could help me.

The next people I met that would influence my healing journey came from the most unlikely source, the church bulletin. It contained an announcement that two women would be speaking at the church Sunday night about healing through chiropractic and guided imagery. It sounded interesting to me so I went to the meeting. Both presentations were very intriguing; so I collected their contact information. Deciding to begin with guided imagery, I called the woman who did this and made an appointment for a session in her house. This would be new territory for me; I'd never done anything like this before.

At our first session she explained to me a little more about the mind-body connection. If I relaxed, and released my negative emotions, I could heal myself naturally. Having read a lot of literature, over the months, that portrayed gynecologists as the enemy seeking to castrate women like me by performing unnecessary hysterectomies, I was willing to try anything to avoid surgery. If guided imagery

28

worked for other people with the right frame of mind it could work for me.

Some of the session was relaxing, other elements were frustrating. She claimed I was holding on too tightly to my emotions. I had to let go and let God and my spirit guides heal me, but I didn't understand what she meant. *Wasn't that what I was trying to do by going through the guided imagery exercises? Why do I always end up feeling bad about myself and that this whole thing is all my fault, and continues to be my fault, because there's something I am not doing correctly to heal myself?* I wanted to scream!

It was as if I couldn't be truthful and acknowledge my own fears or feelings without it somehow having an adverse affect on my body. I was living in a real-life nightmare. Trapped in a place I didn't like, and wanted desperately to get out of, where no one could help me, only myself, and I was failing at it. I didn't blame her I thought the problem was within me; so I made another appointment to see her again. She was friends with the chiropractor, who spoke with her at church, and suggested I might increase my chances of healing if the chiropractor treated me as well. I took her advice. Because both of them worked from the metaphysical angle, I decided to see if this combination would benefit me.

At the chiropractor's office, she gently touched my spine without manipulating my body explaining this would release stored negative emotions. I felt dream-like, rested, and optimistic after our sessions. *"Perhaps this combination would work,"* I thought. Between visits for guided imagery and chiropractic treatments, coupled with my diet, somehow I'd reverse my destructive thinking and be whole and healthy again. All this exploration came at a hefty price tag. These treatments were nontraditional and not covered by insurance. But my health was more important than anything, and I was willing to spend what I could reasonably afford in order to get better.

Before long work became increasingly stressful for me, even more so than my previous recruiting job. Our staff was working overtime soliciting new clients and trying to get our candidates hired before the competition did. Many weekdays I worked until 8 PM, and went into the office alone on the weekends to catch up on email and paperwork. I was living for my job and spending less time with my friends. I still saw them, but not as often. Working so many hours became a convenient excuse for me to avoid dating as much, although I still went out with guys when I met a man I liked.

Often expecting perfection from myself, emotionally and physically, before I could commit to a man, I made dating a low priority in my life. I concentrated on being a top recruiter; receiving many accolades for my performance. That would have to be enough for now. I didn't feel very comfortable with my defective body, and was still too fearful of rejection by any man I liked. It was easier to keep men at arms length until I was ready to expose my heart and life to them. Working so much left me little energy to think of anything else, but I didn't always mind. At least my job was something I was successful at. Working long days seemed like a short-term sacrifice with the potential for long-term gains. If I excelled in recruiting, and made more money, I could take care of myself with or without a man in my life.

In May, I took a much needed vacation with 11 of my former high school girlfriends. We embarked on a Caribbean cruise to celebrate our 40th birthdays. I was the only single one. They'd all been married with children for years. As we celebrated this milestone together, I experienced a lot of mixed emotions throughout the week. Although 40 was becoming an inevitable reality for me, I wanted to avoid calling attention to it more and more. In contrast, my well-meaning and vivacious girlfriends unashamedly proclaimed to other shipmates how old we were, and that I'd make a great catch for any eligible bachelors. Publicly I pretended being single, and turning 40, was no big deal; while privately I mourned. In reality, I was feeling passed over, and ignored, as if it were prom night and everyone else had a date but me. Although I was surrounded by many people I felt lonelier than ever on that vacation. The scenery was beautiful, but I couldn't wait to return to Raleigh and bury my sadness in my work.

Nearly everyone close to me was attached, so I kept relatively silent about my displeasure over my state of singleness. I'd discussed it with friends and family members before, but this time was different. *How do I explain to people my lack of understanding as to why God hadn't answered my prayers?* My situation seemed cruel and unfair to me. All my life family took precedence over a career; I believed I'd make a good wife and mother. Even my friends were stumped. The general consensus of those who didn't understand why some guy hadn't scooped me up yet was that I must be doing something wrong. Therefore, this "condition" of singleness was within my control to change. Apparently, I just didn't want change "bad" enough was the conclusion I came to. As time progressed I started to doubt God's goodness, and my own self-worth. *Maybe I wasn't such a good catch after all. Perhaps I'd done something really awful that brought this curse upon me.* There were many days I viewed being single, and childless, as the worst possible fate imaginable, and that I would never be completely satisfied as a woman if those desires went unfulfilled. Turning 40 wasn't making it any easier either as I watched my dream slipping ever further away from my grasp.

In July, my friends in Raleigh threw a house party for me complete with hula-hoops and dancing into the late night hour. We continued the festivities on a weekend excursion to the Outer Banks of North Carolina where I officially entered my fortieth year of life. The getaway was a great distraction, but the reality of my unchanging circumstances returned shortly after that. Growing more impatient over the lack of progress in my health and love life, I began moving away from mainstream bookstores into New Age ones. I bought tapes on meditation and healing, and books written by women who overcame infertility through holistic means. Traditional and conventional wisdom no longer appealed to me. I longed for a new and different solution.

One day, while driving to work, I heard a psychic on the radio. She was talking to listeners about lost loves; arousing my curiosity. *"Maybe she had an answer for me,"* I thought to myself. As I scribbled her name and number on a spare piece of paper, I remembered I'd heard in church that God said it's wrong to take counsel from psychics. They do not speak on His behalf, but right now I didn't care. I felt like God didn't care either because He wasn't giving me any help or direction. Tired of waiting for a response from the Lord, I wanted to know now how this would all turn out for me.

No one knew I was calling a psychic, not even my room-mate. The psychic lived in California so I'd plan our sessions a few days in advance when my roommate was away. We spoke several times; each session adding a $200 expense on my credit card. That was a lot of money for me, but I was willing to pay it to receive answers about my future. During the fifth session I began to realize this was a colossal waste of time as she pointed me back to a guy in my past; one I had no hope of a future with. She claimed he was the right man for me, and I should pursue him again. All this money I'd spent on a psychic should have been put towards paying off my debt; not incurring more. I was disappointed I still had no real answers and decided not to call her again.

The following week I resumed my guided imagery sessions after taking a month-long sabbatical. The woman I worked with told me I was angry with God; that was why I had fibroids. Although I didn't want to admit it, she was right about my anger. Equally upsetting to me was that I didn't know how to change the way I felt, or who to reveal this to. I was afraid to talk to God about my feelings towards Him; I didn't understand how to communicate with Him. Church attendance and belief in God had always been a part of my upbringing. There was never a time in my life when I questioned God's existence or sovereignty. I'd always practiced the traditions of my faith, and prayed a lot, but lately I was plagued with thoughts that God must be really upset with me. *Why else would He have allowed me to have fibroids as a single woman when I'd wanted to be a mom since I was five years old?* These days, I saw God as the source of my pain; not my Refuge in life's storms, or my Comforter.

This was no new struggle for me. Over the course of my

life, if things were going well I believed God was pleased with my behavior, and I was rewarded accordingly. Conversely, if I did something wrong, He punished me with unanswered prayers. That was how I concluded how God felt about me. Now that it was apparent to this guided imagery mentor, a relative stranger to me, that I was angry with God, I had to face the fact that I was. I wasn't sure who had the answer to my problem, but I knew I had to keep searching for a way to let go of my resentment. Deep in my heart I believed this was the key to my cure, a cure that couldn't come soon enough in my mind.

Chapter 6
The Opening Door

"There you will worship man-made gods of wood and stone, which cannot see or hear or eat or smell. But if from there you seek the Lord your God, you will find Him if you look for Him with all your heart and with all your soul" (Deuteronomy 4:28-29 NIV).

Throughout the summer of 1998 I continued my search as to why things were going wrong in my life, or at least not going the way I wanted them to. Consistently, I compared myself to my wedded and attached girlfriends; mentally storing up perceived flaws as a measure of why I was still single. Somehow I was never thin enough, smart enough, or pretty enough. It wasn't that I couldn't rejoice over my friends. The problem lay in my resentment that I wasn't a wife and mother too. If there was such a thing as karma I couldn't understand why the love I'd extended to others, and the good deeds I'd done, weren't coming back to me in full measure. *Why was I always celebrating everyone else's engagement, wedding, and baby shower, but not seeing my own dreams fulfilled?* I wanted to experience the same things they were and be able to share commonalities again. More than ever I felt I was being left behind in the natural progression of adulthood.

The dating world had recently changed, and I was having a hard time adjusting. Many people were approaching finding a mate similar to looking for a job. There was little room for surprises or the spontaneity that I longed for. I didn't want to make finding a man another project I had to complete, yet many relationship experts stressed the need for a plan. While I knew people who met their spouse through internet dating services and personal ads, I couldn't get excited about taking that route. When a dating dry spell occurred, friends suggested I "do" something different like network more. Ha! If anyone was good at networking it was me! I was not someone who isolated herself from society for long periods of time. *Why did this have to be so complicated?* My hope was simply to meet a man in some unexpected setting.

Although people meant well, the advice that bothered me the most was, "It will happen when you least expect it." *If that was the case, then how do you explain the people doing internet dating? Weren't they expecting to meet someone? Isn't that why they answered personal ads?* I'd never been accused of being desperate to have a man, so why was I being criticized now for voicing my hurt that the right guy hadn't appeared? Instead of getting support from people I felt I couldn't open up to them. No matter which approach I took if the results weren't there it was assumed the problem was with me.

Throughout my life I never needed to have a boyfriend all the time. The simple truth was at 40 I was very ready to settle down. The thought of that not happening, or never having children, was too devastating for me to accept. I never saw myself as an independent career woman putting my job over my family. But I felt I was slowly being pushed into that mold and I didn't want to conform. No career had given me the satisfaction my nurturing heart longed for.

At my next doctor visit my uterus was swollen to the size of a 14-week pregnancy and the fibroids had grown a little. I attributed it to the fact that I hadn't been 100% perfect with the diet or released my negative emotions. The doctor agreed I could continue with alternative healing techniques and surgery should be a last resort. He renewed his commitment to share my methods with other women if I was successful. So I was granted another six months to see if things improved.

My expanding waistline made wearing certain clothes uncomfortable. Still, I managed to fit into my size-four bridesmaid dress for my friend's wedding in Buffalo, New York. We'd met several years early at a retreat while living in Boston. Eventually, she moved back home to Buffalo and I headed off to Raleigh, never losing contact. She was almost 38 and her husband was 41; both were marrying for the first time. They were an inspiration to me that good things can happen to those who wait and don't settle for the wrong person because time is fleeting. Flying back to Raleigh I had a renewed sense of optimism and focus on healing myself. I wanted to be healthy before inviting a man into my world.

Another six months passed, and in early 1999 an ultrasound

revealed my uterus measured close to a 16-week pregnancy. I'd gained 10 pounds and while I felt awful about my appearance I still wasn't ready for surgery. Sometimes I imagined one day I'd be looking at a baby on the screen, instead of fibroids, and be able to say it was worth it to hang on for a new cure. The desire to hold my child in my arms and see the joy on my parents' faces as they beheld their grandchild was so strong, that I was willing to extend my suffering. The doctor cleared me to continue my research, but cautioned time was against me. After setting up my next six month appointment I went back to work in silence.

At home that evening my resentment towards God over unanswered prayers was so strong I collapsed in a heap of tears on my bedroom closet floor. Hardly any of my clothes fit anymore; I wore baggy shirts to conceal my protruding stomach. While I hadn't totally adhered to the diet, who could stay on something so restrictive? For nearly two years I'd considered food the enemy, and that I was poisoning myself if I ate something not on the list of approved foods. I thought crying was bad for me because it was a sad emotion, and felt there was no healthy outlet for my sorrow. All I'd hoped for, and worked so hard for, was crumbling. This couldn't go on; it was time to make some adjustments again.

I stopped seeing the two women who performed guided imagery and chiropractic sessions, and went to an acupuncturist instead. The acupuncturist had an ad about healing female reproductive problems in a local health food store newspaper, and answered my questions specifically about fibroids when I called her. She claimed to have success in this area, so I decided to try this method. During my first treatment I felt a rush of energy go up my arm and out my head. I literally felt like I was standing upside down and defying gravity. *Wow, releasing that much energy had to be good for me!* I looked forward to working with her again; believing I was finally on the right course to healing.

Besides the acupuncturist, there were two additional ads in the same health food store newspaper that caught my eye. The first was a woman who did therapeutic massage and energy balancing. The second was a man who was a personal trainer. Phoning the massage therapist-healer first, I questioned her intently before making an appointment. This was yet another New Age treatment, but she professed to be a Christian and agreed not to conjure up any evil spirits in our sessions together. Perhaps she knew the way to help me reverse my course.

The first massage-healing session was pretty wild and different from anything I'd ever experienced. The woman guided me back in time, and said I was going to break a curse in my family lineage with my thoughts and faith. As she continued talking, I felt pain and heat in my uterus as emotions were pouring out of my body. She told me to envision the fibroids shrinking and that I was already healed in the spirit world. It just hadn't manifested itself in the physical world yet. She asked me to sing a praise song to Jesus, but I couldn't think of any so she sang one for me. After our session I was physically drained but emotionally uplifted. I liked her and knew I'd come back.

Swallowing my pride, I met with my first-ever personal trainer a few days later. The experience was very humbling as he weighed and measured me. I was 14 pounds heavier and confessed it was a combination of my fibroids and recent poor eating habits. I'd rebelled against the strict diet I saw no improvement with and in my disgust, binged on junk food without exercising regularly. I didn't want him to think I was pregnant because I looked like I might be. I was embarrassed about my shape. But he said I wasn't too far gone by any means, and that he could help me.

It was a good thing I opened up and told him about my fibroids because he knew a dietician in Chapel Hill who he'd referred another woman to with the same problem. The dietician helped his referral shrink her fibroids without surgery; she was very happy with the results. *At last, the expert I'd been waiting to meet was revealed!* I thanked the trainer for this information, and was hopeful I'd be her next success story. The dietician agreed to see me but she was only available on weekdays. Chapel Hill was a 30-minute drive from my job, so I had no choice but to break my silence to my co-workers about my health. My boss sanctioned my weekly lunch-hour appointments, and I worked extra hours at night to make up the time.

Everyone in the office was supportive as I declared I was determined to prove this was the way God would heal me without surgery. I still believed I was going to be part of a miracle, and couldn't wait to get my body back into shape. While I was frantically concentrating all my effort on my outward appearance, the Lord was working on my healing from a different angle. Many messengers were about to come my way, and the journey was going to take an interesting turn.

Chapter 7
Wandering from Place to Place

"Remember how the Lord your God led you all the way in the desert these forty years to humble you and to test you in order to know what was in your heart, whether or not you would keep His commands" (Deuteronomy 8:2 NIV).

Throughout the spring and summer of 1999, I had regular appointments with the massage therapist-healer, acupuncturist, physical trainer, and dietician; spending a great deal of money on my health. Fortunately, my commission checks had increased and adequately covered the cost. This led me to conclude I was on the right path because God was blessing me financially. The diet was still strict—no dairy (soy products were allowed), caffeine, sugar, white flour, red meat or alcohol, but it was reasonably manageable. Within four months I'd lost 10 pounds and was feeling more optimistic about my life, even though my abdomen was still hard and a little swollen. I was confident my next doctor visit in late-September would bring good news to celebrate.

Matters of faith were often discussed between me and the massage therapist-healer. In my quest for answers I began to discuss this further with two close girlfriends who were born again Christians. One was a woman I'd relocated from Syracuse to Boston with as part of a company transfer. In Boston, she started attending an evangelical church and told me she was born again. Even though I'd seen her transformation from her formal carnal lifestyle to her new one where she relied on God's wisdom instead of her own, I still didn't think we were different. The term "born again" didn't make sense to me. It wasn't that I didn't have my own vices to contend with, but I considered myself a reasonably good person, and someone God granted a clean slate to each week when I attended church. *At least I'd been making an effort most of my life to live righteously, didn't that count for something? Besides, I already knew Jesus died for my sins, so I must be born again too.* While I admired her new-found devotion, I thought we were the same except she was more of a fanatic than me.

She eventually moved to Oklahoma and attended Bible school before relocating to Atlanta for work. Although we went years without seeing each other, our friendship remained one of mutual encouragement. Over time she became someone I looked up to, often referring to her as my "spiritual big sister". Single like me, she shared how she trusted Jesus to bring her a husband; sometimes mailing me books about faith in Christ. While I'd read what she sent me, it never seemed to sink into my heart. Being a woman of action; not prone to wait on God to give me what I thought I could attain myself, I quickly buried those books away on my shelf; not absorbing what I'd read. Lately, I found I was drawn to them for a second glance.

The other friend I discussed faith and spirituality with was married and lived in New Hampshire. We'd met on a Club Med vacation in 1987 when we were both single. She also shared with me that she was born again and my reaction was the same as it was with my friend in Atlanta. I thought I must be born again too since I was going to church regularly and believed in God. I didn't think there was any difference between us except she was always talking about her faith, and seemed to take it very seriously. I respected that about her and relished in the knowledge that she prayed for me.

In July of 1999 I flew to New Hampshire to visit my friend along with her husband and infant daughter. She was aware I was dabbling in a variety of self-healing methods, and that I believed God was answering my prayers because I looked and felt better. She patiently listened to my tales of restoration through guided imagery and self-discovery without expressing her views. While driving to the beach, I heard a song on a CD she was playing that I liked. When she said the CD contained a variety of Christian artists I was shocked. *"What? This can't be Christian music."* It sure didn't sound like anything I'd ever heard in a church. It was contemporary, upbeat, and fun. I always thought listening to Christian music, outside of a church service, was boring. Discovering I could like these contemporary Christian songs was a new revelation.

When I returned to Raleigh and met with the massage therapist-healer, I asked if she knew of any contemporary Christian artists. She recommended a few, so off I went to

43

the Christian bookstore to listen to CD's before buying any. Their music and message energized me, and I thought this must be one more piece of the puzzle to aid in my healing. With all this positive energy in my life, eating the right foods, exercising regularly, and believing in myself I just had to see a difference at my next doctor appointment! No one I knew put more time into their health than me; something had to start working soon.

Approaching my two-year battle against fibroids, I flew to New Mexico, in late-August, to visit my friend and fellow soldier in this medical war. She complimented me on my progress while offering continued support against this enemy seeking to rob me of my perceived God-given privilege—the right to bear children. Our friendship deepened as we spent the week traversing New Mexico; delighting in the adventure. Until now, I had no idea what a beautiful state it was with its varied terrain. I fell in love with it. Surrounded by mountains as far as the eye could see was soothing to my soul. Days later, my feet touched down on Raleigh soil as my heart beat with renewed vigor. I was certain victory was eminent, and that I was nearing a turning point.

I was right, there was a difference when I went to see the doctor in late-September, but the difference was not what I expected. The fibroids were larger. After my appointment I called the dietician and trainer and shared the news with them, and decided to stop seeing them. The acupuncturist and the massage therapist-healer were the only people I saw on occasion. After all the time, money, and energy I'd invested, only to have the fibroids be worse, my discouragement ran deep. The hardest part was that this problem I'd wanted to keep so private had become very public. I felt defeated; yet I still couldn't resign myself to undergo surgery and not have it work out the way I wanted.

Although hope gleamed in encouraging words courtesy of family and friends, it quickly faded to gray as feelings of isolation crept in. How I burned to hear from another woman who'd triumphed holistically in her war with fibroids. Hard as everyone tried, no one could understand my plight. Some offered consolation by claiming all this suffering was character-building. That statement only sparked my melancholy. *What was so wrong with my character in the first place?* Without any explanation as to why this was happening, all I could do was hope 2000 would be better than 1999.

A few months later, I ushered in the new millennium with an optimistic spirit. I saw 2000 not only as a history-making event, but another fresh beginning. Just before the holidays, my roommate moved out to live with her fiancé and a new roommate took her place. Born in Turkey, she was adventurous and an extremely interesting conversationalist. I was fascinated by her decision to leave her homeland and come to America. It was one thing for me to have lived in different states, but I had never set up residence in a foreign country. I admired her bravery. We both had a wide circle of friends and lived somewhat separate lives, but also planned activities where both sets of friends intermingled. It was a happy environment and great having her company.

As my living conditions stabilized, so did my financial obligations. Despite all the money I'd spent on my healthcare I'd managed to reduce my credit card debt to a balance of $10,000. In February I contacted a bank representative who allowed me to consolidate that balance onto one credit card with zero interest due until the end of August. Being debt free was at last within my reach, and although it was a lofty goal, I aimed to make enough money to pay off the balance before the August due date.

By April I decided to change jobs again. Maybe it was God testing my faith, but since I began tithing ten percent of my income in January my commission checks had dropped significantly. This was the first time I'd ever tithed and did so expecting a great blessing from heaven. But the harder I worked at my job when everyone else in the office had gone home, the more the hiring goals I needed to achieve eluded me. As fate would have it, a former recruiter I'd worked with when I first came to Raleigh called me about contract employment with two firms in Research Triangle Park. They were both top national employers, and presented a great opportunity for me to move into corporate recruiting.

I agreed to interview with both of them and received subsequent offers on the same day! It was a hard choice, but I accepted the one that was the most challenging and the opposite of any recruiting assignment I ever had. I'd be working with a team of recruiters traveling throughout the United States hiring employees nationwide. The employer of the company, whose offer I declined, told me to keep in touch with her in the event I was looking for work in the future. This would later prove to be a valuable contact for me.

By the time I gave notice of my departure to my current employer, my earnings were 50% less than the previous year. This made my upcoming contract assignment even more appealing. With a higher salary I'd be able to make up some lost ground financially and that was encouraging. Once more I had a new beginning to celebrate. It was reinvention time again for me as I started my new job the week of Memorial Day. With a short learning curve, life quickly became a whirlwind of activity for me and I loved every hectic minute of it!

I was part of a national recruiting team hired to bring onboard 1200 people by the end of July. The team was energetic and cohesive, and I was valued by management for making a significant contribution to our goal. Traveling each week had its perks. Not only did it break up the monotony of sitting at a desk and staring at a computer screen all day, but I often worked in cities where family and friends lived; squeezing in short visits. With all the overtime I was working, the money was pouring in faster than I could spend it. Before long the day arrived when I paid off my credit card balance in full, and I was debt free for the first time in years. What a big relief! Now I could concentrate on replenishing my long-neglected savings account, vowing to never abuse credit cards again.

My social life was improving too. When I wasn't traveling I spent more time with my friends. Weekend excursions included trips to Charleston, South Carolina, and backpacking in Linville Gorge and Roan Mountain, North Carolina where I hiked part of the Appalachian Trail. Three of us trained all summer and completed a 64-mile bicycle race in Hillsborough, North Carolina in August. At the end of September we celebrated the marriage of my former roommate in Chapel Hill.

I was more socially active than I'd been in a long time, and was making more money than ever before. My recruiting job was the best I'd ever had, and I loved going to work. Other than my health challenges, life was good.

Now that I'd mastered my finances, I was feeling very confident and ready to take a chance at dating again, hoping to find the happiness I'd been seeking for so long. Fearing rejection, I'd been silent about telling a past love what my true feelings were for him. Inside I had this nagging sense the time was fast approaching for me to express my admiration in the hope that he'd reciprocate. This was uncharted territory for me being the one to speak up before the guy did, but I felt I was being led there. *Maybe it was God pushing me to speak so I'd hear the answer I'd been praying for*. Little did I know the conversation was about to change the course of my life.

Chapter 8
Taking it to the Edge

"For He knows the way that I take; when He has tested me, I will come forth as gold" (Job 23:10 NIV).

Sessions with the massage therapist-healer continued while those with the acupuncturist ended. With limited time for appointments, due to my travel and work schedule, I had to make a choice between the two. The massage therapist-healer reassured me the fibroids were shrinking and evidence of such would soon manifest in the physical world. Her conviction kept me coming back for more. The New Age self-help sources I read were in agreement that I had brought this medical condition upon myself as part of my spiritual journey. Because I chose this path I controlled my own destiny, and the outcome of my healing. How I longed to pass this test before me, but there seemed to be no quick fix.

Grasping at any formula that offered a cure, I began combining holistic with traditional remedies. After reading an article that taking birth control pills sometimes shrank fibroids by regulating the estrogen that caused them to grow, I asked my OB/GYN to prescribe a low-dose pill for me. I had a new doctor now after the previous one moved out of state. When I showed her the article, she was doubtful the pill would work due to the size and number of my tumors. But she agreed to prescribe it and would measure the results in a few months. *"How ironic,"* I thought to myself. *"While most women take the pill to prevent pregnancy I'm taking it in hopes of one day being pregnant."* Still not ready to surrender in my battle to preserve my fertility, I remained optimistic this would be the magic cure combined with my massage therapy treatments.

Regular meetings with the massage therapist-healer always made me feel relaxed and comforted. Whenever I divulged my inner struggle to understand God, she recommended Christian authors to read. The books she suggested talked about being healed in my heart first through a personal relationship with Jesus. I had heard this before, but didn't really understand what that meant. Still approaching things from the outside perspective, I continued striving in my own strength to do things I thought were pleasing to God to gain His acceptance. In my mind, the only time I was "right" with Jesus was when I behaved correctly. I wanted to be close to Him, and longed for peace in my soul, but thought it was only possible by my own doing; not anything God could give me.

My curiosity about having a close relationship with God was further peaked when friends of mine began attending various evangelical churches in Raleigh in search of joining one. The denomination I grew up in definitely stressed a reverence and fear of the Lord, but not a personal relationship with Him. The term "born again" was never used, and individual Bible study was not encouraged, although the Scriptures were preached at every service. As long as I could remember, I felt something was missing and talked with many church members about this void in my spirit, but no one was able to help me. They'd just look at me and say, "You must love the Lord very much." I thought that I did, but never felt peace with God like my born again evangelical friends did. Knowing I was searching, my friends invited me to go to service with them.

The group was looking to join a church that offered Bible studies and programs for singles. We visited several churches each Sunday over a month or so and discovered we all liked Providence Baptist Church. Their sermons were alive with practical applications for daily living as the preachers walked us through Old and New Testament Scriptures. I was amazed that most people brought their Bibles and notebooks to each service. This was a whole new world for me; it felt as if I were attending a university class and learning God's Word.

It was so much more than facts the pastors where sharing. With simplicity and reverence they illustrated how the Bible is God's living Word and contains life's instructions for every generation, not exclusively for people that lived over 2000 years ago when Jesus walked among them. At the end of each worship service, the pastor said if anyone wanted to learn about having a relationship with Christ, or join the church, you could speak privately with two deacons who would answer your questions. I wasn't ready to walk forward yet, but decided to keep attending service with my friends so I could hear more.

In early October, on a business trip in Florida, I received a long email from a guy I'd dated four years ago and hadn't heard from in a few months. Even though our relationship was brief, his impact on my heart was long lasting. I'd always kept a special place for him in my heart, and wished we'd dated longer. He'd broken up with me when he met someone else, but we'd remained friends who communicated a few times a year. Whenever we spoke our conversations lasted for hours, and he always made me laugh harder than anyone I knew. He was the same guy I'd recently felt I should reveal my desire to date again now that he'd been unattached for awhile.

A job change had taken him away from Raleigh in 1999, but that didn't stop us from staying connected. Recently, he'd shared with me that he had accepted Christ as his Savior. Upon hearing this, I had the same reaction as when my friend in Atlanta told me she was saved when we lived in Boston. I thought it was just a phase. Both these people were fun-loving, liked to party, and didn't care much for attending church like I did. They were prone to alcohol and food addictions, and struggled with mood swings. I thought they were using Jesus as a crutch because they were weak and had traded one addiction for a new one— religion. Still, I couldn't deny both of them were different. Something profound had happened to them and they were not the same. Their addictions no longer had a stronghold on them, and they weren't as anxious about life as they used to be.

This guy didn't even talk the same way he used to. His interests and desires had changed; he spoke with such love and confidence about how Jesus had done this. I wanted to know more, I wanted what he had. This was not the guy I knew before. I found I was more attracted to him as he shared things he was learning from God. It seemed we'd both been on a journey of healing and discovery these last few years apart, and now the timing was finally right for us to be together.

Sitting in that Tampa hotel room my eyes devoured his words; absorbing every morsel with great delight until his note proclaimed the news that he was in love. He'd recently begun dating a divorced mother of two who was also a Christian. Immediately, my haughty attitude reared its ugly head as I thought to myself, *"Is he crazy? How could he be in love that fast? Doesn't he realize what's in store for him? Why would he choose her when he could have me with no ex-husband and kids to worry about?"*

Grappling with this explosive news, my heart was pounding as my mind struggled to reject it. *What about all those times he was so excited when I called him; telling me I'd made his day? Did I imagine the affectionate greetings we exchanged?* Over the years, the dance of words between us continued endlessly without leading anywhere. Because I liked him I kept participating; wanting it to be real, not some fantasy I was chasing. He'd kept me in his life without committing anything. *Maybe it's my fault; he doesn't know how I truly feel.* Our paths had crossed so often these last four years I'd assumed it was fate, or unfinished business between us. This charade had to end; I couldn't pretend being friends was good enough anymore.

Equally petrified of rejection as I was of a renewed and committed relationship with him, I didn't know which frightened me more. Because he lived out of state, he hadn't seen me recently and was unaware of my health problems. Still, if he really cared for me nothing could separate us. It was now or never; I had to let him know what had transpired between us. While not intentionally disingenuous, he was a skilled angler; reeling me in with each tasty word he cast. *How best to approach him? Do I call him? No, I'll stutter in fright, never articulating correctly. Wait, I'll write to him! This will give him time to think things over before responding. Perfect!* Pensively I composed my email explaining my nervousness, and my confusion over our conversations. Esteeming him on his strong work ethic and how appealing that was to me, I shared my desire to date him again. Noting his relationship with Christ had a profound impact on my faith walk, I thanked him for sharing his thoughts with me. Shaking as I pressed send, I was hopeful he'd reciprocate soon and that God would turn his heart back to me.

A week went by with no response which I interpreted as a good sign. If he'd replied quickly I would have known he hadn't taken me seriously. When his reply appeared in my inbox later that week, I held my breath as I started to read it. The first few sentences were sensitive in nature. He acknowledged how hard it must have been for me to write to him, and that he was sorry he didn't respond sooner. He needed time to think about what I'd written. My heart was racing as my eyes combed his words searching for signs of his affection. I was grateful he'd thought about this before replying, and was waiting to read good news. Without warning his tone changed, and he said the harshest words a Christian could probably ever hear. God was about to use him as a messenger to open my eyes to my own sinfulness.

In strikingly blunt fashion, he proceeded to tell me I worshipped him more than God. *What? How could he say that? He'd completely misunderstood my admiration for him. It was never meant to be worship, but encouragement and edification. This can't be true that I've made him into an idol and looked up to him more than God!* As if things couldn't get any worse, he said I was an example of how sin hurts others and has far-reaching consequences. He confessed it was his sin of lust for me, and that he did not love me. While he'd been physically attracted to me in the past, these last few years he'd considered me a friend and nothing more.

His final words emphasized that we should end all contact with each other immediately, and that I should not write back. So that was his reply. No apology for hurting me; no kind words to easy my pain. Just a note that ended harshly saying I should not respond even if I felt tempted. I'm sure I scared him, but I didn't mean to. What a crushing blow! I would have liked a gentler landing back to earth, but I had gone to the edge, and jumped off the cliff without thinking, and the landing broke my heart. My spirit was wounded and humiliated; I felt more cast-aside than I'd ever felt in my life.

Sobbing uncontrollably that night as I packed for a weekend backpacking trip, in western North Carolina, I turned my wrath toward God. "Why did I have to meet this guy? I don't understand if you're a loving God why you don't answer my prayers with happy relationships. You know how many times I've been disappointed by men. Why did you allow another disappointment to come into my life?" I recall yelling Psalm 37:4 to God, one of the few passages I knew. "It says if I follow you you'll give me the desires of my heart. So why are you denying me all the time what's in my heart? Haven't I done more good things than bad in my lifetime? Don't I put out more right thoughts and actions than evil ones in the world? Am I such a wicked person that I never deserve to have a husband and children? If you gave me this desire only to torture me I don't want it anymore!"

My grotesque onslaught against God continued as I approached the pinnacle of self-pity. "How could you allow my health to deteriorate? Why did you afflict me when I've been so observant of good nutritional practices for years? It's not fair that I'm suffering while others who abuse their bodies are not! Don't you care about the pain I'm in? It can't be true that I subconsciously brought on this illness. Who in their right mind would will this into their life? As one of the walking-wounded I'm no longer capable of offering advice; I can't stand my body!"

The rage poured out of me that night like a dam bursting from the current. It was the worst anger I'd ever expressed, and it felt like it was years in the making. All the frustration over unfulfilled dreams was coming to a head and rushing like a waterfall running over a cliff. I couldn't contain my hurt anymore, and while I knew putting God's character on trial was wrong, I didn't know what else to do with these feelings. All I could hear over and over again were those haunting words from the man I wanted to date again, "You worship me more than God." How do I defend that accusation? Even more frightening and seemingly impossible to admit, what if he's right?

Chapter 9
Moving on Again

"Come near to God and He will come near to you. Wash your hands, you sinners and purify your hearts, you double-minded" (James 4:8 (NIV).

The weekend backpacking trip afforded a plethora of convenient distractions. The forest was afire; adorned in various shades of red, amber and green which made for a striking contrast against the cloudless blue sky. With no close friends accompanying me on the hike, I could be relatively quiet, introspective, and unnoticed—just as I intended. This outing club trip was part of my physical conditioning to ready me for a 10-day trek next month in the Grand Canyon. Throughout the day, I mulled over my lost love's words attempting to convince myself of his error. *How could showing my devotion to his goals and dreams be worship?* But as I mentally revisited former conversations between us, I gained some insight into his perspective. Craving his admiration, I'd refined my interests and dreams to mirror his. From his vantage point, I was building an altar with his name on it as priority number one in my life. This was a destructive pattern I'd been repeating for years with other men.

Whenever I learned the longings of my love interest's heart, I'd commence adjusting my lifestyle to please him often compromising my own moral beliefs. My entire self-worth was contingent upon his opinion of me; so when our relationship ended I over-personalized it; blaming myself for its dissolve. For months (in some cases years) thereafter, thoughts of regret consumed me as I imagined mistakes I'd made and longed for another chance to prove my worthiness. Because of this, I labored to move on into a new relationship even though my date already had. With astounding frequency, I was too enraptured by the appearance of things, and my feelings of emotional bliss, to have a clear and discerning mind about our relationship. I knew this one was over for good, but I had to have the last word.

Fresh from my weekend in the mountain air, I decided to call him. About to hang up when his voicemail recording beckoned me to leave a message, I began my semi-rehearsed speech with a tinge of nervousness in my voice. Claiming empathy, I said I understood his feelings differed from mine, but I believed he'd misunderstood my intentions. As a passionate person, I care deeply about things I consider of great importance; my compliments were never meant to imply I was worshipping him. Attempting to redeem my reputation and convince him I wasn't a stalker, I apologized for making him feel uncomfortable; promising to end all contact hereafter. Wishing him well, my shaky hand placed the phone back in its cradle. The door to the room he'd occupied in my mind had closed. In time my heart would shut him out too.

Travel for work continued to increase and my manager suggested I apply for a passport. He predicted some international travel for me in the near future. I'd been selected the designated recruiter to attend job fairs, trade shows, and interview days we conducted. This was welcomed news to me. I'd really begun to savor mixing up the time I spent in the office with interacting with people directly. There were days traveling so much was tiring, but overall this was still my favorite job and a great match for my extroverted personality. Going to different parts of the country energized me and allowed me a mental break from my personal cares and concerns.

Before I could apply for a passport, things took a sudden turn. I received a phone call at home, one Friday night in late October, from the account representative who'd helped me find this contract position. She told me the company, whose stock price had been hit hard earlier that week, was going to lay people off starting with contractors. The recruiting staff would be reduced as hiring was frozen and cancelled in some departments. Because I was a senior recruiter on the team, and paid the highest hourly rate, this put me at a disadvantage under present circumstances. I was the first one on the team to be released.

What shocking news! I couldn't believe the job I'd loved so much was now over. The account representative assured me they'd been very happy with my performance. For my service I'd receive two-weeks of severance pay and a great written reference. They said it was strictly accounting, nothing to do with me, and they were very sorry. I felt awful about losing this job. However, in the next breath, she told me the most unbelievable news that calmed my fears around looking for one to replace it. Earlier that day, she'd called the manager of the company I had interviewed with five months earlier, whose offer I declined, and let her know my contracted ended. She asked the manager if she had any openings and if she'd reconsider hiring me as a contractor for her team. The manager had two openings and offered one to me. I'd have to wait a week to start because she didn't have a phone or computer for me, but if I accepted the offer she'd have things ready when I arrived.

Amazing! What perfect timing to have another offer from a company I'd declined five months ago. The hourly rate was slightly lower than what I'd been making, and there was no travel or overtime with this job, but that was okay. At least I was employed with a good salary and benefits package. Thanking the account representative for all her hard work, I agreed to start my new contract on November 6th as they'd requested. It was a relief I didn't have to start my new job for 10 days. Right now I felt like a member of an athletic team who'd just learned I was traded to another team. It would take me a few days to remove my old team jersey and shift my allegiance to this new organization. I was unsure of this new job, and wasn't exactly thrilled about sitting at a computer again all day, even though I was grateful to be employed. But I kept telling myself everything happens for a reason and maybe one day I'd understand.

In the last month, I'd stopped attending church regularly as I was often out of town on the weekends. Although I really liked Providence Baptist Church, I still went back and forth between various churches without making a decision to join any of them. Life was so chaotic; I wanted something stable. Part of me wanted to remain with the denomination I'd grown up in with its comfortable familiar doctrines and traditions, and another part of me was restless and wanted to know God in a way I'd never known Him before. I wasn't satisfied staying where I was, but I was scared to completely let go and trust where I was being led. I decided to do nothing for now.

The first week of my new job, my manager approved my unpaid trip to the Grand Canyon. I didn't mind that as a contractor I wasn't eligible for paid vacation for several months. It was great having the flexibility to take time off as long as it wasn't too great of a hardship on the rest of the team. Funds had been plentiful the past six months of my contracting career, and I'd replenished my savings account with ample cash for trips, shopping excursions, and emergencies. Even though I had enough money in savings to carry me for six months financially, I remained frugal never forgetting what is was like to be overextended.

Initially apprehensive about my new environment, the transition progressed with relative ease. My co-workers were extremely welcoming, and those of us who started on the same day helped co-train each other. Still in touch with my former colleagues, I was able to tell them I was adjusting quicker than I'd expected. Hearing rumors of their own future release, I offered to keep them abreast of any recruiting positions I heard of. Although I missed many aspects of my former employer, I was grateful for my current position.

As November progressed, I was no longer mourning my lost love and previous job. Rather I was looking forward to the challenge of hiking for 10 days and seeing the Grand

Canyon for the first time in my life. I also wanted to spend time doing some soul searching. Although I didn't know in-depth details of many stories in the Bible, I did know God often led people into a desert when He wanted to do something powerful and drastic in their life, or when He wanted to reveal something to them. I was ready to go explore that physical desert having felt I'd been in a spiritual and emotional one for the past several years. I longed for refreshment and relief; perhaps I'd find it in that arid climate.

Chapter 10
The Mountains in the Desert

"Come, let us go up to the mountains of the Lord...He will teach us His ways, and we shall walk in His paths" Micah 4:2 (NIV).

On the morning of November 18, 2000 I boarded a plane to Las Vegas, Nevada with three people I barely knew. Once in Las Vegas, we'd rent a car and drive five hours to the south rim of the Grand Canyon and begin a 10-day backpacking excursion. All three of them had hiked in the Canyon before and were well acquainted with the terrain. I was the only novice who'd never done a backpacking trip beyond the mountains of North Carolina, but I wasn't worried about going with them. We were all members of the ski and outing club, and they seemed like nice people.

Two weeks prior to the trip, the leader assembled us and advised what we should pack for our hike. Whatever we packed in, we had to pack out; there was no trash collection service in the Canyon. He told us women to be prepared with ample feminine supplies because strenuous hiking could trigger heavy bleeding. My period ended well before the trip, but I packed a few tampons as a precautionary measure. I feared my greatest nuisance would be handling the pressure of uterine fibroids on my bladder. This hike wouldn't be easy under the best of conditions, but I wasn't going to let anything interrupt this once in a lifetime experience.

While in flight I gazed out the window in amazement over the size and beauty of the Canyon. Thoughts raced through my mind of how God created and sustained everything on this marvelous planet, and that somehow I'd lost sight of that truth. Over time, I'd adopted the belief that God remained relatively uninvolved in life unless provoked. As I pressed my face against the airplane window, a stream of tears ran silently down my cheeks and I admitted to myself that I didn't have a heartfelt relationship with God. I only had an intellectual one that came from preconceived notions in my head. I was scared of God and therefore my actions towards Him were born out of duty, and not love. I didn't have an inkling of what delighted Him or how I fit into any great plan of His.

I felt so sad and quietly prayed to God about these matters in my heart. *Please God, give me heart knowledge of you. I don't really love you. I'm afraid of you and scared to approach you. I want to know and understand what it's like to ʾoved and accepted by you. I'm tired of always trying to ʾmething to make you happy, tired of trying to make ʾice me. I feel so angry all the time. I want to have my soul and feel your love inside of me. I don't*

64

*know how to get that kind of peace and keep it. L
do only brings temporary happiness. There's ,
something more than just existing. I want to live ,
pose. Please help me.*

There was no measurable change in me after I prayed, but a
verse came to mind that encouraged me to press on in my
quest. Jesus extends the invitation to come to Him and
promises He will reveal Himself, "So I say to you: Ask and
it will be given to you; seek and you will find; knock and
the door will be opened to you. For everyone who asks re-
ceives; He who seeks finds: and to him who knocks, the
door will be opened" (Luke 11:9-10 NIV). It was still a
mystery to me how this happened, but I could feel Jesus
pulling me closer like a strong magnetic force. My resis-
tance only increased the tension between us, and I knew it
was I who was holding back, not He. In my fear of losing
my own identity I wasn't ready to let go and be joined to
Him. So I decided to pray for more assurance and wait to
see how Jesus answered my prayer.

We arrived at Bright Angel Lodge where we savored our
last night of indoor sleeping and dining for awhile. At sun-
rise, we boarded a bus and embarked for Hermit's Rest
trailhead. There was no turning back now—into the desert I
headed with great anticipation and enough adrenaline to
conquer anything! It took us nine hours to descend straight
down halfway into the Canyon where we made our camp in
the dark. My headlamp battery had burned out, and I could
barely see where I was pitching my tent. It was a long and
restless night for me. With temperatures in the twenties I
couldn't get warm no matter how much wool and fleece I
wore. When morning came, and I surveyed my surroundings, I noticed I'd slept with a ram's skull beside my tent.

What an interesting greeting that was!

As we hiked down to the Colorado River, my quadriceps shook for seven hours until we reached the base. While setting up my tent I started bleeding as if I had my period. I was hoping the bleeding was temporary. Perhaps the two days we'd spend by the River before our next strenuous trek would make it stop. At least we were near a stream where I could wash my clothes and myself. The water was a frigid 47 degrees but it was better than having no water at all! This was a good place to replenish ourselves; we were all grateful for the rest.

Cold and alone at night in my tent, I often cried thinking about the homeless. I'd chosen this existence for a designated period of time, and would soon return to a warm apartment with all of its modern conveniences (especially indoor plumbing!) at my fingertips. Others had no such choice. *How could anyone survive in harsh weather 24x7 for months on end?* Until now, I'd never seriously contemplated their painfully difficult reality, which sharply contrasted my everyday luxuries, and sensed this was a fortuitous trip; no ordinary vacation. Daytime provided little relief from the elements and while the Canyon was beautiful, it was nonetheless extremely challenging. With a myriad of fibroids, it was like carrying a bowling ball around inside of me, and I couldn't escape discomfort. The bleeding persisted after I'd depleted my tampon supply. My only option was to wear a folded-up wash clothe that I rinsed in the River daily. *Oh, those poor pioneer women who preceded the invention of sanitary products!*

Later in the week, we crossed a suspension bridge over the Colorado River into Phantom Ranch. It was so beautiful with campsites and cabins nestled in the gold-leaved Aspen trees, and a stream where deer drank. There were no showers but the indoor bathrooms were equipped with sinks. What joy! This was luxury camping compared to what we'd endured all week. After spending the night, we hiked towards our next destination, Indian Gardens on Bright Angel Trail. All around us the scenery was breathtaking, especially when we traversed the Tonto Plateau. The colors were captivating and even though it was cold we enjoyed crystal blue skies. Our trip was coming to a close and Indian Gardens would be the last place we'd sleep inside the Canyon walls. While I couldn't wait to get back to my own bed, I knew I'd miss these incredible surroundings.

Early next morning we began our ascent. We started on the winding trail known as the Devil's Corkscrew. That day I was hiking faster than the others, so the leader released me from the team, knowing we'd reunite at the rim. Before I left he asked me to carry some garbage in my backpack. It belonged to my female counterpart who was having knee trouble, and the men had no room for it in their packs. My initial response was to joke about how it wasn't fair that I had to transport her garbage just because I was in better physical shape. *Didn't I deserve an easy hike out considering I'd prepared well?* So much for my reward! Now I was being asked to sacrifice for the group and I didn't like it. While I did agree to carry her garbage, my attitude was all wrong.

When I was a safe distance from the others, remorse set in. I realized how selfish I was. Marching through the Canyon dust, I was embarrassed that my initial response was to reject my teammate in her time of need. This incident revealed a side of me I didn't want to admit existed. When put through the paces, I wasn't the team player I portrayed myself to be. Lately, my life felt like walking in a forest during winter where nothing is concealed anymore. Parts of my personality, crouched behind a lush tree in bloom, were previously hidden until the winter winds stripped the foliage away; revealing what the leaves had masqueraded. For years I'd covered myself with compliments, the niceties of others tossed my way when I'd done something perceived to be honorable and good by them. When fiery trials burned through my combustible temperament, the façade crumbled and the ugly interior was exposed. I could no longer pretend to be righteous. I was weak and sinful and longed for transformation.

Looking back, I saw the fires I'd faced were God-ordained and my heart began to agree with the words of King David, "It was good for me to be afflicted so that I might learn of your decrees. The law from your mouth is more precious to me than thousands of pieces of silver and gold" (Psalm 119:71-72 NIV). All my previous sacrifices were not pleasing to God and couldn't make amends for my sins. Only Jesus as a holy and blameless sacrifice could do that on my behalf. I'd heard this message preached many times, "For God so loved the world that He gave His one and only Son, that whoever believes in Him shall not perish but have eternal life" (John 3:16 NIV), but until now it never penetrated my being what Jesus did out of love for me.

As I continued hiking, I felt God reassuring me of His love, and I suddenly remembered the first time I heard about being born again from a seminary student in 1983. He shared the Gospel with me and I proclaimed I'd accepted Christ into my heart, but it wasn't a true surrender of my will. There was no evidence of any transformation in my heart or lifestyle after that announcement. I made the confession seeking the approval of the seminary student, not the indwelling of the Holy Spirit. Yet despite my waywardness, God continued pursuing me and inviting me inside His world. He promised I'd still be able to exercise free will, but as I spent time communing with Him, I'd notice my desires changing. If I allowed God, He would give me new hopes and dreams for my life, and the power to fulfill them by His Holy Spirit. He would sustain me in suffering and celebrate life's joys with me. All that happened to me would be for a divine purpose and an ultimate good.

So on that crisp November day in that majestic physical desert, in one solitary moment my fear of the Lord flowed out of my body as fast as my feet were propelling me upward. I was laughing and crying simultaneously when I invited Jesus to live in my heart, and He removed me from my spiritual desert. I told Him, *"I don't care if I have to live in a tent the rest of my life I'm yours!"* I felt more alive than ever and keenly aware that this was the start of a whole new life for me. The peace and contentment inside me was indescribable!

Once at the rim, I waited 45 minutes for my teammates. This worked to my advantage and allowed me time to collect my thoughts. It was cold and icy and I felt strangely out of place with all of the tourists mulling around. People were wrapped in warm clean clothes and I looked every bit the ragged hiker that I was. It wasn't long before someone spotted me and exclaimed, "Oh look, a real backpacker!", as if I were a park tourist attraction. I laughed and told them not to stand too close since I hadn't showered in awhile. When the others arrived we had a group photo taken of the four of us. This was a trip we'd never forget, especially me!

Chapter 11
Starting on a New Path

"Call to me and I will answer you and tell you great and unsearchable things you do not know" (Jeremiah 33:3 NIV).

By the time I returned to work in Raleigh it was December 1ˢᵗ. What a wonderful way to have spent Thanksgiving in the Grand Canyon, and to come out of there as a brand new creation in Christ Jesus! I didn't make any formal announcement to anyone about surrendering my life to Jesus. But I did say the trip was the most challenging getaway of my life, and that it opened my eyes to a lot of things. Ready to make a serious commitment to studying God's Word, I called Providence Baptist Church. Speaking with the singles pastor there, I learned about their singles gatherings on Wednesday nights, and a women's Bible study on Monday evenings. I registered for a singles ski retreat planned for January in Wintergreen,

Virginia, and anticipated making new friends while inviting my current friends along.

December was packed with many fun activities. My Turkish roommate was not a practicing Muslim and had no objections to celebrating Christmas. So we had a Christmas party with 30 guests, including the three people I'd hiked with in the Grand Canyon. Everyone was fascinated by our adventure as we exchanged photos and relived the experience for others to hear. I still couldn't believe I'd done the trip with so little backpacking experience prior to going!

The following weekend we went skiing in Boone, North Carolina with several ski and outing club friends. There I met three people who invited me, and my friends, to join them in a singles Sunday school class they attended at Providence Baptist Church. How fortunate to meet people who were attending the church I was looking to join! We exchanged contact information and agreed to stay in touch. One of my girlfriends from the ski and outing club wasn't sure how she felt about God. But she found our conversations about faith intriguing, and decided to go to church with me. Before long she was attending weekly worship services with us and accepted Christ as her Savior too.

Celebrating Christmas and New Years in Syracuse with family and friends, I recapped my Grand Canyon adventure for my captive audience. Walking around on an emotional high, I was in denial over my physical deterioration. I'd been bleeding for a month. By January, 2001 I knew I couldn't fight this anymore, and wasn't capitulating because I lacked faith. I still believed God had the power to miraculously heal me. I'd recently seen such a story in the Bible. "Just then a woman who had been subject to bleeding for 12 years came up behind Jesus and touched the edge of His cloak. 'She said to herself,' "If I only touch His cloak I will be healed". Jesus turned and saw her. "Take heart, daughter", He said, "your faith has healed you." And the woman was healed from that moment" (Matthew 9:20-22 (NIV). I so wanted that to be my story, but I could no longer pretend being healthier emotionally was translating into physical wellness.

In fact, I was much worse. My protruding stomach was hard to the touch, and I frequented the bathroom every 30 minutes. *What had I done to myself by waiting so long?* Because the decline happened slowly over the last three-and-one-half-years, I'd grown accustom to feeling tired; I'd forgotten what it was like to feel good. My kidneys hurt more often, and I never slept uninterrupted. I still went on the church singles ski retreat in Virginia, but was very uncomfortable, and didn't spend much time on the slopes. No more avoidance, it was time to contact my doctor to discuss surgery options.

When I called about scheduling an appointment, the office assistant said my doctor had left to start her own practice; she wasn't seeing patients until May. I couldn't wait that long and asked, "If you were going to have surgery which doctor in the group would you choose?" She thought highly of all of them, but suggested a new doctor that could see me at the end of February. Accepting her recommendation, I decided not to tell anyone until I knew when the surgery was scheduled. Hopefully I was still a candidate for a myomectomy instead of a hysterectomy. Even though I felt lousy, I still couldn't bare the thought of the later.

At the end of January, I joined a women's Bible study class

that met Monday evenings at Providence Baptist Church. We were studying Proverbs, and I couldn't believe how practical it was! Words written thousands of years ago were just as applicable to my life today. I was learning that all Scripture is God-breathed. Because the Holy Spirit directed the biblical authors to write God's words of revelation to them, along with what their eyes witnessed, the words will always pertain to all generations throughout history. God ordained what would be written in the Holy Bible, not men. The writers were only instruments used by Him.

My desire for studying God's Word, and learning daily application of it, drove me to read anything I could get my hands on pertaining to this. Stories written by authors who shared what Jesus Christ had done in their lives greatly encouraged me. I wanted to nourish my hungry mind and soul with the right food, delicacies that God was serving. I'd write Scriptures on index cards that particularly touched my heart, and kept them in my car to read at stop lights. As I meditated daily on God's Word, and memorized some of the verses, I felt like a radically different person; a calm spirit. While I still experienced the ups and downs of life, I was no longer on an emotional rollercoaster. What a relief!

Through continuous study of God's Word, I was learning much about the depth of God's love for me. No longer were His commandments burdensome to me. I saw them as liberating me from sin, and protecting me from harm. With the Holy Spirit helping me to lead a holy life, I didn't have to try in my own strength to keep His commandments. I just had to lean on Jesus who wanted to help me. My desire to move closer to God was so strong it was slowly flushing out my fear of His anger when I sinned.

I knew He hated sin, but He didn't hate me. When I confessed my sin, and repented of it, He quickly forgave me.
No longer did I strive to change my behavior. Instead, I
presented all of me to Jesus, and prayed He'd mold me into
the woman God wanted me to be, not what I thought I
should be for God. Christ's loving presence was helping me
change from the inside out first; soon my behavior would
reflect this. None of my circumstances had improved, but
my attitude had, and life became full of endless possibilities
again. Everyday was a good day as I looked forward to
what the Lord was going to teach me next.

Chapter 12
Time to Choose

"For I am about to do a brand-new thing. See, I have already begun! Do you not see it? I am making a way in the desert and streams in the wasteland" (Isaiah 43:19 NIV).

In February, I attended a seminar for anyone interested in joining Providence Baptist Church. I knew the next step for me was to be baptized, and discussed this with two of the deacons. They asked me some questions to confirm I believed that Jesus Christ was my Lord and Savior. Convinced of my sincerity, they agreed I could participate in the March baptismal ceremony. They explained that the pastors only baptized individuals able to articulate their salvation is in Christ alone. Baptism is an outward sign of their inward commitment. If their belief was not heartfelt, then baptism was simply a ritual not indicative of being saved. I took this very seriously, and knew this would be my public declaration of my soul's conversion. I was very excited about my decision, and joining Providence Baptist Church.

There was another choice I had to make, and the day arrived to do so. It was February 27th as I sat in the examination room waiting to meet the new OB/GYN I'd discuss surgery with. Silently I prayed and asked the Lord to reveal His plan to me. If there was any reason I shouldn't work with this doctor, I prayed God would make it obvious to me today. Minutes later, the doctor and nurse walked into the room and introduced themselves. The doctor asked what my concerns were and I explained I'd been struggling with uterine fibroids for nearly four years. Despite various methods I'd used to heal myself I wasn't better. I said it was time to make a decision about surgery.

Needing to conduct an exam before making a surgical recommendation, the doctor appeared convinced my fibroids were only visible on an ultrasound screen. *Naturally. My oversized sweater and loose-fitting skirt provided an adequate disguise, even to a trained doctor's eye.* As I lay back on the table; lifting my sweater, his opinion quickly changed as he responded to my bulging abdomen by saying, "This is very bad, Mary." Helping me up, he warned of possible kidney failure without surgery. Unable to predict the time table, but certain of the outcome, surgery was my only option to remove the fibroids, and rid my body of their stress.

By his calculations, my uterus measured the size of a 20-week pregnancy; the cut-off point for performing a myomectomy. Because of the severity of my case, he recommended a hysterectomy, asking why I'd waited so long. My response was something along the lines of not having enough faith in the outcome, and the inability to trust God until recently. Before I could utter another word the doctor replied, "I'm a Christian too, Mary, and God uses many methods of healing." He said Luke was a physician who meticulously recorded, in his gospel, the various miraculous healings he witnessed Jesus perform. There wasn't just one method. Each contained God's divine fingerprint and intended message He sought to convey. At that moment, I knew our meeting was God-orchestrated.

As we closed, he asked if I wanted to go home and pray before making a decision. I declined, telling him with conviction in my voice I knew he was the physician the Lord selected for me. Once more I did not waiver in my choice of surgery. I requested a myomectomy stating that I couldn't make the choice myself that I'd never have children. Even though I knew the odds were against me, giving up now and resigning myself to a hysterectomy felt like concession when I was so close to victory. I wasn't going down without a fight, and I wanted a doctor who was willing to battle with me. Against his better judgment, but agreeing to do his very best, my surgery was scheduled for April 19th. I left his office with a sense of peace knowing I'd made a wise decision.

The time had come to tell my family, friends, and co-workers about the surgery. There was no reason to be secretive anymore. After my doctor visit I was able to share that God heals people many different ways, and that my previous failed attempts were serving a good purpose in my life. The Lord used all of what I'd gone through to humble me, and draw me close to Him. Jesus wanted me to trust Him, and let Him take responsibility for my healing, so He would get the glory; not anyone else. As I re-read the story about the woman with the issue of blood in Matthew 9:20-22, I found more details in Mark's account. "She had suffered a great deal under the care of many doctors and had spent all she had, yet instead of getting better she grew worse. When she heard about Jesus, she came up behind Him in the crowd and touched His cloak, because she thought, 'If I just touch His clothes, I will be healed.' Immediately her bleeding stopped and she felt in her body that she was freed from her suffering" (Mark 5:26-29 NIV).

Wow, it was like reading my own story! I too had spent most of my savings seeking healing from all kinds of sources while trying to keep my sickness hidden for fear of being shunned by men. But God had a different plan. While I was not about to experience a healing without surgery as she had, I believed God was calling me to step forward so many could witness Him work in my life. Although it wasn't the kind of miracle I'd hoped for, Jesus was enlightening my heart to trust whatever way He healed me would be spectacular in its own way, and His will for my life. Now that I'd made my surgery choice I thought my faith, and trust in God's power, was strong. But the next seven weeks would be a time of great testing, and I would soon learn if that were the case.

Chapter 13
My Isaac Moment

"The Lord will guide you always; He will satisfy your needs in a sun-scorched land and will strengthen your frame. You will be like a well-watered garden, like a spring whose waters never fail" (Isaiah 58:11 NIV).

P rior to my baptism on March 18th I prepared a short testimony on how I came to know Jesus as my Lord and Savior. Every time I thought about what to say, the same Scripture came to mind describing how God used many trials to bring me to the point of confessing my sin, my need for forgiveness, and asking Him to save me. "Brothers, as an example of patience in the face of suffering, take the prophets who spoke in the name of the Lord. As you know, we consider blessed those who have persevered. You have heard of Job's perseverance and have seen what the Lord finally brought about. The Lord is full of compassion and mercy" (James 5:10-11 NIV).

Standing in a side-room adjoining the altar, I was a little nervous about sharing my testimony, but felt better hearing others speak before me. My roommate and a dozen friends were among those seated in the congregation that Sunday night. As I walked up the steps, into the warm waters of the baptismal tank on the altar, excitement replaced my fear about speaking. *Outside of getting married, this is the biggest commitment I'll ever make as I dedicate my life to Christ.* I publicly shared how God had tested me in my relationships, finances, and health. Even though my circumstances hadn't improved, my attitude had because I had joy in knowing I wasn't alone. I closed by quoting James 5:10-11. The head pastor held me as he took me back under the water to signify my death to sin and burial in Christ, then raised me up out of the water to show my identification in Christ's resurrection, and new life in Him.

The only response I could utter in that moment was, "Yes!" People were laughing and clapping as I walked out of the water into the backroom of the church to change into dry clothes. With none of my family living nearby, it was great to have the support of my friends who witnessed my baptism. My roommate wasn't able to join us for dinner afterwards, but later that evening in our apartment we had a great conversation about what she'd seen. God was planting seeds in her life too, and teaching me that these events in my life were not solely about me. They were His way of pointing people to His Son, Jesus Christ.

By the time April arrived, I was exhausted night and day. Suffering from sleep-deprivation, I awoke hourly to go to the bathroom, and my kidneys were often sore. With surgery just weeks away, I went to the lab for my preoperative blood work, feeling strangely out of place. That day every

patient around me was old and extremely frail. I knew illness and pain played no favorites, and that no age group
was immune, but I still couldn't believe I was part of the
unhealthy population considering how healthy I used to be.
The scale revealed I was 24 pounds heavier than three-plus
years ago when first diagnosed with fibroids. That was a lot
of weight for a small-boned person like me, and added to
my discomfort.

Awaiting the results of my preoperative tests, the doctor
cleared me to fly to Cleveland for a friend's wedding. At
the end of the weekend trip my period started and something happened to me that'd never happened before. When
I used the last tampon my period stopped. Usually I'd have
some leftover supplies for next month or would have to buy
more because I'd run short for this one. I'd never depleted
my exact supply at the same time the bleeding stopped.
*Maybe this was God's way of preparing me for a hysterec-
tomy?* Since I couldn't be sure, I didn't buy anymore supplies and decided to see what the outcome of my surgery
was.

Ten days pre-surgery I met with my doctor to discuss my
blood work; receiving an ominous report. I was severely
anemic and he wanted to postpone the surgery. He feared I
might bleed-out during the operation and suggested a hysterectomy. There I was, pushed to the edge emotionally and
finally at my breaking point. Call it stubbornness, or just
sheer determination to overcome every obstacle and negative statistic facing me, I elected to pass on his suggestion.
With a trembling voice, I said I couldn't make the decision
that on April 19th I'd lose the ability to have a baby. A hysterectomy was too permanent of a solution for me; I wanted
him to try to save my uterus. The doctor was concerned

how I'd react to the news of having had a hysterectomy if one was required to save my life. Regardless of the risks, I said I wanted to place it in God's hands; let Him decide. At least this way I wouldn't have to wonder what might have happened if I'd trusted Him instead of reacting out of fear.

With some hesitancy, the doctor agreed and wrote me a prescription for iron supplements. Immediately, I began taking massive doses and consuming iron-rich foods. We wouldn't know if this raised my iron levels until my test results the day of surgery, but he was willing to try. That was all I asked. Later that evening I drove to the home of one of the women in my Proverbs Bible study. Our small group was having a fellowship to share what we'd learned in our study, and to exchange prayer requests. When my turn came I told the group about my lab results, and asked them to pray my iron levels would increase before my surgery. As we said our goodbyes, one of the women walked outside with me and asked me how I was doing. Tears streamed down my face as I told her I was tired, scared, and weak in my faith. Instead of agreeing crying meant I lacked a strong faith she said quite the opposite was true.

She said Jesus knows this is a great sacrifice for me, and a huge leap of faith to trust Him to determine the outcome. One day when I meet Jesus in heaven I will hear Him say, "Well done good and faithful servant! You have been faithful with a few things; I will put you in charge of many things. Come and share in your Master's happiness" (Matthew 25:22-23 NIV)! Like an angel's voice straight from heaven those words comforted me, and I thanked her for sharing them. We parted ways and I drove off into the darkness, anxious to get home. I'd had enough drama for one day. Before falling asleep God gave me another Scripture to reflect upon. "I will lead the blind by ways they have not known, along unfamiliar paths I will guide them; I will turn darkness into light before them and make the rough places smooth. These are the things I will do; I will not forsake them" (Isaiah 42:16 NIV). Reading that verse, I knew I was on a God-ordained journey.

This was no ordinary path I'd been traveling. While I was a brand-new creation in Christ, I was not a finished product, and there was more pruning ahead. *Pondering the circumstances of my life, perhaps God's desire was that I remain single; unable to bear children. Maybe I'd work in ministry helping other women like me find joy and love in Jesus.* But in order to be a minister of Christ's love to others, I had to be a recipient who trusted Him; one who was willing to exchange her dreams for His plans. While I'd put up a gallant fight to preserve my dream of motherhood, maybe it was time to let it go. In the silence of my little apartment bedroom, I prayed for clarity, and felt God asking me to surrender having children completely. My response to Him became my very own "Isaac moment" of trust. "Take your son, your only son, Isaac, whom you love, and go to the region of Moriah. Sacrifice him there as a burnt offering on one of the mountains I will tell you about" (Genesis 22:2 NIV).

Just like Abraham had to trust his son's life to God, I had to trust my body, and purpose in life, to the Lord as well. Without hesitation I began praising and thanking God for all He'd done for me. Since He created my uterus He controlled it, and I offered it back to Him. Undoubtedly I'd grieve if I had a hysterectomy, but I knew that night He'd help me through the pain. If suffering is what it took for God to bring me to repentance, and to know Him intimately as I do now, then it was worth it! Having the power of the Almighty God living inside my heart, and working in my life, was better than anything I'd ever known. I wasn't going to allow earth's temporary dreams take my focus off my real source of satisfaction in life, Jesus.

So willingly and cheerfully, I raised my hands to heaven and released all that I'd held onto so tightly for 42 years. For the first time in my life I completely trusted God was good, and that He acted out of love. No longer was I a salmon swimming upstream fighting against the current of life. I was in a solid boat with the best Captain anyone could have, Jesus! He would not let the waters of this storm overtake me, or any other I'd face. This was more thrilling than any of the white-water rafting trips I'd done before, now that Jesus was my guide. He'd tell me how to paddle around the boulders, and how to navigate treacherous rapids and waterfalls. I could almost hear Him say, "Come on Mary, let's go down this long river together. There will be moments of calm waters, and times of turbulent waves. You may even get tossed out of the boat and wonder if you'll be hurt or killed. But remember what I told you, and get back in the raft with me. Let's have an adventure together that will be truly exciting!" With that thought I said, "Okay Lord, I'm in!" "Get ready", He said, "the ride is about to begin."

Chapter 14
Rejoicing in Suffering

…"Not only so, but we also rejoice in our sufferings, because we know that suffering produces perseverance, perseverance, character, and character, hope. And hope does not disappoint us, because God has poured out His love into our hearts by the Holy Spirit, whom He has given us" (Romans 5:3-5 NIV).

On the morning of April 19th I awoke with so much peace about my surgery I couldn't wait to go to the hospital! Many people were praying that day, and I felt God's angels encamped around me. Mom and I arrived at the hospital around 7:00 AM, courtesy of my roommate, where my mother was allowed into the prep area with me. It was like watching a well-choreographed routine as the nurses moved swiftly and gracefully around me; preparing my body for the surgeon. They tested my blood and with a reading of 9.0 I was still anemic, but the surgery would not be postponed. Good! No more hesitation; no more bargaining for additional time. I was ready to have this ordeal over with, and to begin healing.

One of the nurses started my I.V. with an antibiotic that made me feel warm and itchy within minutes. My mother didn't notice anything, but when the nurse returned to check on me she said, "Oh boy, this isn't good." These were definitely not the words I wanted to hear prior to major surgery! Evidently, I'd broken out in hives in an allergic reaction to the antibiotic in the I.V. Immediately, she switched my medications and the hives began to recede. *Given all the opposition I'm facing, something good must be on the horizon because Satan is trying so hard to prevent this from going well.*

A few minutes later a man from my church entered the room; asking if he could pray over me. What a nice gesture to reach out to a new congregant like me. True, I was on several prayer lists but our church has thousands of members. I didn't expect anyone on the outreach ministry team to know about me, or what hospital I was in. What a great comfort to me, and my mother, to have this kind man pray for me. We thanked him and shortly after that it was time for me to go. My mother kissed me as she whispered that it would be all better when I came out of the surgery. I felt sad for Mom. It must have been hard for her to see her child going into surgery no matter how old I was.

As the nurses wheeled me into the operating room my legs were shaking. Reality had set in. The thought of being cut into and operated on was not easy to accept, even though I trusted my doctor was a capable surgeon. While the team strapped my arms and legs into place, the doctor leaned

over me as he held my hand. He asked me how I was doing. My response was to ask him if he'd prayed about this
surgery. He said he prayed every morning. "Okay then," I
said, "just tell me how many fibroids there were when I
wake up. I'm ready now." Gazing at the clock on the wall,
it read 9:40 AM when I felt myself drifting off and said,
"Oh boy, here we go," while the doctor was still holding
my hand.

Sometime mid-afternoon, I awoke in the recovery room
during a blood transfusion. There are no words to adequately describe the amount of pain I was in. The closest
analogy is to say I felt like I'd been sawed in half. All this
time I never worried about the physical pain of this surgery.
My focus was always on the emotional. Within seconds,
the doctor was holding my hand as he said, "We removed
18 fibroids; the largest being the size of a grapefruit. Others
were as big as apples and oranges. Smaller ones we left in
place because they were so tiny; we don't believe they'll
bother you. You've lost a lot of blood and are having your
second transfusion, but we saved your uterus. Your fallo-
pian tubes and ovaries looked great; you should heal up
nicely." *Did I just hear him correctly? No hysterectomy?* I
looked up and whispered, "Thank you," then drifted off to
sleep again.

Groggy from medication, I vaguely remember riding on a
gurney in the elevator towards my room. My mother was
beside me as the nursing staff transferred me from the gurney to the bed. Knowing how much I wanted to avoid a
hysterectomy, she was crying tears of joy that my prayers
were answered. I asked her not cry anymore because I
couldn't cry. The incision was so painful I had to keep my
emotions in check for now. That wasn't very hard under the

present circumstances. I was incredibly weak, and void of the energy to express them. Severe anemia had rendered me helpless; leaving me without the ability to do anything for myself. I was like a newborn baby again; entirely dependent on my mother for assistance.

With a catheter in me inserted during surgery, I never left my bed those first 24 hours. Whoever invented the catheter I'd like to personally thank them! The thought of any movement, particularly getting out of bed, held no appeal to me. Right now it even hurt to breath. Taking inventory, it was hard to fathom all the monitors attached to me. There was some type of apparatus squeezing and releasing automatically around my ankles to prevent the development of blood clots, and I was wearing an oxygen mask. This was the most invalid state of my adult life, and panic set in if my mother left my side for more than a few minutes. Being defenseless, I didn't want to be left alone.

Starting my morphine drip line, the nurse inquired about my pain level using a graduated rating from 1-10. Previously known for my high pain tolerance, I couldn't seem to admit the severity; so I whispered a nice mid-range number—six. In reality, it felt more like 16! Assuring me it was impossible to overdose no matter how often I squeezed the line, she completed her instructions on its usage. Without exaggeration, the morphine had no numbing affect on my pain. *Maybe this was a placebo?* Regardless, I never mentioned my discomfort to the nurse. Concerned about over-medicating myself despite her proclamation, I decided to endure the pain knowing one day it would end.

Due to anemia and medication, it was impossible to quench my thirst. Every time I saw the clock read five minutes versus 25 minutes since my last sip of water, I was stunned. Unable to lift the cup to my mouth, my poor mother was commissioned to aid me. Currently, we were polar opposites. She was freezing in the air conditioning; wearing her jacket constantly while I ran a fever; insisting the heat was on. The catheter was removed by the second day, requiring me to get out of bed for bathroom visits. Mom assisted me in and out of bed; rubbing my trembling legs that shook uncontrollably after each trip. I worried I might be wearing her out, but she never complained. Struggling to recover, I took a downward turn; prompting a third blood transfusion when my levels reached a dangerously low 5.0. Pale as my bed sheets, my appearance frightened Mom. *Am I a wimp? I never thought it would be this hard. No wonder some people don't rebound from major surgery.*

One night, as I lay there in agony, the only audible sound in that dark hospital room was my own labored breathing. The pain was incessant and in the still silence I thought, *"Death would not be a bad option right now."* Certainly I didn't want to die in that instant, but I could now sympathize with suffering people who'd lost the will to live. Yet beyond the pain, I felt God's presence soothing me; bringing my soul contentment. As bad as this was, it dwarfed in comparison to Christ's suffering during His crucifixion. Fixing my mind's eye on God, I was able to temporarily transcend my pain as I became acutely aware He was supplying the life-giving strength I needed. As I savored His touch in that moment I required nothing. In the grand scheme of life, this was such a short time to be out of commission. God would help me flourish no matter how long it took.

All of a sudden I was so appreciative of life. It was as if my senses were more alert than ever before. I couldn't believe what a miracle it was that God created us with the ability to survive many kinds of infirmities. From that moment on, I knew I'd get through this because my strength was not in myself, but in God's healing power that I was tapping into. My attitude became one of thankfulness--thankful for the gift of health, my family and friends who loved me, the doctor and the nurses who cared for me, and that I was part of a miracle. Over the last four years I'd been limiting God; believing the only way He could heal me miraculously was apart from surgery. But the Lord had humbled me through this season of suffering. Because my search for a cure was a story I was forced to share publicly, God brought glory to Himself through this surgical method of healing. He touched the lives of so many people who didn't give me much hope for anything other than a hysterectomy.

While I didn't know what the future held for me, it didn't matter so much to me anymore if I got married or stayed single. What mattered most was pressing onward toward a deeper love relationship with Christ, and serving Him with all of my being for the rest of my life. "…for I have learned to be content whatever the circumstances. I know what it is to be in need, and I know what it is to have plenty. I have learned the secret of being content in any and every situation, whether well fed or hungry, whether living in plenty or in want. I can do everything in Him who gives me strength" (Philippians 4:11-13 NIV).

Chapter 15
Less of Me and More of Jesus

"So we fix our eyes not on what is seen, but what is unseen. For what is seen is temporary, but what is unseen is eternal" (2 Corinthians 4:18 NIV).

On Sunday April 22nd I was still anemic at a level of 6.5 when my doctor said, as he held my hand, that I'd do better at home under my mother's care. I was so swollen from the I.V. fluids my mother had difficulty dressing me, and squeezing my feet into the shoes I'd wear home. Every part of me was aching when my roommate asked, as she drove us home, "After all of this are you sure you still want to have kids someday?" *That was the last thing on my mind!* I didn't want anyone touching me. Knowing future births would require I have a cesarean section, if it hurt as much as this surgery did then I'd remain childless. The only thing I wanted was to get to the apartment and take a shower. Mom and I hadn't bathed in three

in a lifetime partnership now. I was satisfied just *being* in His presence and not *doing* anything, but resting and healing. All this suffering had a purpose. In time, God would reveal how He wanted me to console others with stories of what He'd done. Nothing created a sense of urgency in me anymore. At last, I was taking things one-day and one-step at a time.

Not only was it a tremendous help having my mother with me for a month, it created a strong bond between us. We'd always gotten along just fine, but we'd never been through a long stressful experience as this surgery was. Much to my delight, no problems surfaced between us. Near the end of her stay, Mom attributed our positive experience under trying conditions to my constitution. She noticed I reacted differently to stress than I used to growing up. I was no longer an emotional basket case tossed about by life's unpredictability. God was my anchor and that assurance not only calmed my spirit, but allowed me to rejoice in whatever the day's events contained.

At my three-week post-surgery visit, the doctor expressed his satisfaction with my progress. While I still had a long way to go, the worst was behind me; I was moving in the right direction. When asked, he replied the reason I was still in pain was because many muscles were stretched during my surgery; the delicate repair work performed on my uterus was more invasive than a c-section birth. I was in the top 5% of women with the most number of fibroids he'd ever removed, and that most surgeons attempt to remove. Not a good category to be in. Even he was amazed he'd been able to save my uterus. He cleared me to return to work part-time in early June, saying he'd see me again in three weeks. What a gift from God this visit was, and so nice to walk out of a doctor's office smiling after so many years of hearing less than optimal news!

The day arrived for my mother to fly home to Syracuse, and for me to be moving towards self-sufficiency. I was very sad to see her go, but couldn't be selfish. She had to return to work and other family obligations. Just before Mom left, another former college roommate, this one lived Rochester, New York, called offering to come and stay with me. She assumed I would still need help after my mother left. She was right, and I accepted her offer. In addition, many of my Raleigh friends (including the guys) offered to use their vacation time to stay with me, or run errands during the day once Mom went home. I was overwhelmed by their generosity, and it comforted my mother to know she was leaving me in good hands. What a blessing to have so many loving people in my life; so many angels God had sent my way at a time when I needed help most.

It was so good to see my former college roommate when she arrived in mid-May. I knew we'd have some thought-provoking, and heartwarming, conversations while she was with me. My current roommate was very welcoming to her, and they got along famously. The two of them entertained me with funny stories accompanied by great Middle Eastern and Mediterranean cooking. We also spent time at the home of our mutual college friend with her husband and their four boys. It was great reminiscing about our school escapades, and catching up on current family events. Such a welcomed treat for me to get out of the apartment for a few hours, and I enjoyed every minute of it!

The following morning my boss called inquiring about my

progress; delivering the news that hiring needs had sharply dissipated. Spared from the previous month's downsizing the second round of lay offs had begun; this time affecting me. As a contractor, I'd been absent on unpaid medical leave; ineligible for sick pay or a severance package. Prior to surgery, I'd saved several thousand dollars anticipating out-of-pocket medical expenses, but was always planning a hasty return to work. Before closing, she asked if I'd received the five paid vacation days I was entitled to. Because I hadn't, she'd submit a request for this and advised me of my unemployment benefits. Knowing I could file for unemployment assistance was a bonus I hadn't counted on. Pledging to stay in touch; offering me help whenever she heard of a job opening, we ended our conversation. Though short-lived, I was grateful for the new business connections I'd made in her organization.

As my Rochester friend packed for her flight home, I shared the news of my job loss. My calm demeanor convinced her it was good news in disguise. While unemployment would pose some financial challenges, I'd just been granted additional recuperation time. *Perhaps God was prompting me to explore less volatile career options. True, this was another test in the midst of many upon me, but how could I be unnerved?* Basking in the warmth of God's bountiful grace these recent months, I lacked no good thing. As it was, I enjoyed a better earthly lifestyle than Jesus did when He became flesh. Although not privy to vast sums of wealth or material possessions, I was being asked to relinquish all to its rightful owner, God. Life was no longer about playing it safe; concentrating on my own self-preservation. *What was my assurance in?* My reaction to these trials would answer that question definitively.

Chapter 16
Praying for My Husband

"May the Lord continually bless you with heaven's blessings as well as with human joys" (Psalm 128:5 NIV).

Five weeks post-surgery, I attended a singles retreat over Memorial Day Weekend at Fort Caswell, North Carolina. Longing to see how God would use His teaching vessels to communicate to me, He wasted no time capturing my attention. It started with the opening lecture when the guest speaker reacquainted us with the story of Abraham's test of faith, through the sacrifice of his son Isaac, and posed a thought-provoking question. "What is God asking *you* to give to Him and trust the outcome?" That was easy; I had a laundry list of items! Finding employment was a primary concern since my recent downsizing from my corporate recruiting job. Continued healing from major surgery was a vital need I trusted God to supply. But more than any other petition, I believed God was asking me to lay my desire for a husband and children on the altar, and leave it there for Him to determine the outcome. *Ouch!*

Previous attempts made by me to deposit this precious request at His feet were not left unattended by me for long. In moments of impatience, I'd hastily remove it from God's presence, and make another futile attempt at fulfilling this dream in my own strength. At nearly 43-years-old, it wasn't getting any easier for me to wait on the Lord's answer to marriage, and motherhood. Desiring not to repeat my past actions, I told God I wanted to react differently going forward, and to have the faith of Abraham, faith that would spur me on in radical obedience. So I prayed for my will to be aligned with God's, and that He would help me release this dream completely, trusting that the answer He revealed would be the best one for me.

As we gathered in small coed groups throughout the weekend, it encouraged me to hear other believers share their challenges and victories in their walk with Jesus. When the retreat ended, our leader handed each of us a bookmark with a Scripture that was unique. Mine read, "May the God of hope fill you with all joy and peace as you trust in Him, so that you may overflow with hope by the power of the Holy Spirit" (Romans 15:13 NIV). Sadly, I was disappointed; preferring a verse that contained a reference about love as if that would affirm a man was in my future. *How foolish I was seeking only to hear from God what I wanted the Word of the day to be!* Clearly, Jesus was telling me to put my confidence in Him. With a repentant heart, I crawled on my knees before his altar, and committed to trust His plans for my life. I knew whatever happened that God would prepare me for it, and see me through it.

In early June, I attended an information session for women interested in our church's mentoring program. While I continuously profited from the teachings of our pastoral staff, I coveted a one-on-one relationship with an older Christian woman. A week later I met my mentor. She was 60-years-old and we shared some commonalities. We were both born in Upstate New York and raised in the same religious denomination. Like me, she'd suffered through the pain of fertility challenges, and validated my longing for children later in life. She was told she'd never conceive, but after adopting three daughters she bore two sons in quick succession, the youngest after 40. Her story inspired me, and I sensed the weekly three-month commitment we'd made to gather would have a lasting impression on me. I could hardly wait to see how God would touch my life through this mentor He'd chosen!

In addition to my mentor, God presented me with another opportunity to study His Word. He reconnected me with a group of women I'd met at the singles retreat in May. They invited me to join their summer-long Bible study held every Monday evening at one lady's townhouse. Their invitation was good news to me, and an obvious indication that the Lord was feeding my spiritual appetite from many sources; I happily accepted. There was a spirit of camaraderie amongst us from the first night. Our group was composed of five single women and one newlywed. Although we hardly knew each other, all of us were eager to learn together. The study's main focus was on finding your significance in Christ, and developing the mind of Christ. We'd read various Scriptures, accompanied by daily homework questions, and share our answers each week. I was enthused to learn from Jesus about my identity in Him, and what it meant to be His disciple.

Before we left, the leader asked us to share prayer requests. When my turn came, I blurted out with no reservation the first thing that came to mind, "Let's pray for men!" I couldn't believe I was so bold! But my heart was so ready to see God work in my life, and in the lives of the other single women, that I couldn't hold back. The leader agreed and enthusiastically replied, "If we pray for them, God's going to send them!" Everyone laughed as we concluded our gathering, and I smiled as I walked out the door to my car. I could tell from the leader's response that she had great faith in God's abilities. Her conviction that He would most certainly answer us convinced me we'd all soon be dating.

That was a pivotal night for me. My heart contained more than a glimmer of hope; it was filled with a raging fire! With Jesus as our advocate, the Father would hear our cries, and yesterday's dashed hopes would be replaced with tomorrow's happy endings. Now that I'd publicly announced my desires, it was time to begin praying for men to cross my path. Discussing this with my mentor a few days later, she confirmed if God hadn't removed my desire to marry, He must have plans to fulfill it. I'd granted Him full access to change my heart if it wasn't His will for me to be a wife. Since He hadn't squelched the dream, I trusted He was still working on making it a reality.

In a phone conversation with my friend in Atlanta affectionately dubbed my "spiritual big sister", I shared I'd been asking Jesus to send me a mate. Her reply seemed rather unconventional in nature, and it pushed me off-kilter when she suggested a different approach; one that she, as an over-forty single woman, had adopted. While it was perfectly reasonable for me to pray for *a* husband, she said I should pray for *my* husband as if I'd already met him. "How do I do that?" I asked her. "How do I pray for someone I don't know yet?" She explained that praying for my husband today allows the Holy Spirit to create a spiritual bond between us that would be self evident tomorrow.

The more I pondered this new way of praying, the more I embraced it, and asked her to tell me more. Scripture affirmed her words, "Now faith is being sure of what we hope for and certain of what we do not see" (Hebrews 11:1 (NIV). She suggested I begin by praying for his faith, protection from evil, and for his character to be Christ-like. This wasn't an exhaustive list, but enough to inspire my soul. While I likened these prayers to learning a foreign language, it came from my trusted sister in Christ who always gave sage advice. So I thanked her for sharing with me, and committed to praying for her future husband too.

The next time I met with my mentor, we talked about praying for my husband as if I already knew him. She agreed that praying for Jesus to touch someone else's life, always released blessings into our own. While it was no guarantee I'd receive everything I prayed for, that wasn't what I was seeking. Before I was born again, I thought I had to "earn" God's favor, but learned quite the contrary was true. The Lord wanted to "give" me His favor; not because I was good enough, but because He is great enough! It's one way of expressing His love for me. What pleases God most is when we are not afraid to ask Him and believe what He sends us is perfect, regardless of the packaging the gift is wrapped in. "The Lord delights in those who fear Him, who put their hope in His unfailing love" (Psalm 147:11 NIV). So along with my girlfriends who were praying for men, my mentor partnered with me to seek God's blessing and be watchful for His favor. What a sweet journey of surrender to Jesus this was becoming!

Gradually, my prayers became more directed. Unaware who my future husband was, or the circumstances of his life, I prayed general blessings such as: that he was a man of integrity who loved and feared the Lord, protection over his job, and for Jesus to prosper the work of his hands. If unemployed, I prayed for the gift of work and the monies to meet his obligations. Being fun-loving and family-oriented, I asked for a like-mate and that we'd be compatible in all areas: spiritual, emotional, physical and financial. My greatest hope was that our union would be one of mutual encouragement; filled with maximum grace and minimal strife. Above all else, I wanted a happy and peaceful home; one that honored our heavenly Father who gave it to us.

In addition to praying for my future husband, I prayed I'd be a good helpmate to him, "A wife of noble character who can find? She is worth far more than rubies. Her husband has full confidence in her and lacks nothing of value. She brings him good, not harm, all the days of her life" (Proverbs 31:10-12 NIV). With the help of King Jesus, I could become of a wife of nobility to my husband. Lastly, I prayed God would quicken our hearts for each other. I wasn't asking Him to rush us into marriage, but rather that He'd confirm quickly whether or not we should keep dating. I'd grown weary of false promises uttered to me by former companions, and tired of being hurt. If he wasn't God's best for me, I wanted immediate discernment, and the discipline to end our relationship gracefully. With complete security in God as my matchmaker, I pledged to wait patiently for my spouse. Who better than God to choose him? Jesus knows what challenges lie ahead, and who would be a good partner to face them with. My hope was no longer in my ability to work the laws of attraction to my advantage, but in God to give me favor in a man's eyes.

Over my lifetime when things disappointed me, I would cry out to God in anger. Like a demanding child, I wanted to know *why* what initially brought me happiness tragically turned into sorrow. Now that my heart belonged to Jesus, I saw endless possibilities for my life. God's Spirit replaced my negative questioning with His positive truth, and slowly I began to proclaim, "Why not me?! If it's God's will, He'll bring it my way. And if not, it's because He loves me and has something better in mind, even if it's single-hood." At last I was free from the impulse to take charge of my life! This wasn't a license to wander lazily throughout my days, but rather to share my God-given talents and let Jesus be my provider. It was such a powerful and adventurous way to live; just as He intended it to be.

As my prayer life deepened, the Holy Spirit imparted me with a joyful heart, and I commenced praising God for His gift of salvation while I was still single. Now that I was God's adopted daughter, I wanted my husband to be part of the same family, and so did God. He knew for me to marry outside His will, by joining myself to an unsaved man, was to subject myself to great trials and tribulations. As always, God's Word of warning was for my protection. "Do not be unequally yoked together with unbelievers. For what fellowship has righteousness with lawlessness? And what communion has light with darkness" (2 Corinthians 6:14 NIV)? Knowing what type of man God wanted me to marry I wasn't going to step outside His loving boundaries. As our group prayed in accord for God's blessing, I assumed I probably wouldn't be the first bride. I was the oldest and while we were all vivacious and attractive women, youth was their advantage. Although my childbearing years were fleeting, God gave me hope that He could make a way through my obstacles too. "What is impossible with man is possible with God" (Luke 18:27 NIV). Amazingly, before June became July God answered my humble prayer, giving me a glimpse of His humorous side, by sending me men through some comical channels. The summer of 2001 was about to become the summer of love for me in more ways than one!

Chapter 17
The Rain Begins

"I will send down showers in season; there will be showers of blessing" (Ezekiel 34:26 NIV).

M y next doctor visit brought more satisfying news. While still swollen and sore around the incision, my muscles had recovered from their state of atrophy. No longer anemic, I was gaining strength as I shed 19 of the 24 pounds I'd been carrying. Fearing caffeine, including chocolate, might escalate the growth of the fibroids left untouched by my surgeon, I avoided it altogether. Never again did I want to relive this painful ordeal. Having completed all of my post-operative exams, the doctor released me from his care. Unless I developed any complications, my next appointment would be in a year. *Praise God!* Sharing the news of my success with the massage therapist-healer, I thanked her as we parted ways; promising to keep in touch.

Before long, God began stirring up my dormant love life again. The first raindrop in the shower of men Jesus would send appeared in my apartment complex leasing office. I caught the eye of one of the tenants renewing his lease, and he stared with intrigue as I entered the room. His eyes were wide-open as if I was dressed impressively, but my outfit was a simple pair of shorts with a sleeveless shirt. We exchanged hellos and a smile, but nothing more. After he left, I sat down with the same leasing agent and extended my own lease before returning to my apartment. I'd already forgotten about him, but apparently he was thinking of me. That afternoon, the phone rang and the leasing agent asked if she could give him my contact information. Initially, I was caught off guard but she assured me he was really nice; so I gave her permission. He called shortly afterwards, saying he'd like to take me out to lunch, but he was unemployed. No shame in the truth, we had something in common! Collectively, we decided to meet at a restaurant and split the cost of a buy-one-get-one free sandwich.

We drove separately and met outside the restaurant entrance. Over lunch he divulged he was a Christian whose faith was important to him, and he wanted to be honest with me. He was attracted to me, but was unsure how involved he wanted to get. He'd just ended a relationship and was considering relocating out of state if he found work. I was comfortable being friends and had no illusions about anything more serious right now. Because I was traveling to Syracuse with my roommate the week of July 4th, he said he'd call me when I returned. Later at home I thanked God for the date as I prayed for wisdom. Just because he was a Christian didn't mean he was the right man for me. In our summer Bible study group we kept each other accountable for our actions, especially concerning men. I was learning more about what God says our relationship with Him should be, as well as dating relationships. My entire concept of God, and attitude towards Him, was ever-evolving as I replaced the lies I'd believed for so long, lies that Satan had whispered in my ear about God being disappointed with me, with the truth about *who* I was in Christ. No longer was I *doing* things to get God to approve of me, or love me. Because I'd accepted God's free gift of grace through faith in His Son Jesus as my Savior, God saw Jesus when He looked at me now. I was redeemed, and approved by the Father, and wanted to respond to His love by honoring Him with my daily life choices.

Since Jesus is the physical representation of God the Father on earth, looking at Him afforded me a glimpse of God's character, "I am the way and the truth and the life. No one comes to the Father except through me. If you really knew me, you would know my Father as well. From now on you do know Him and have seen Him" (John 14:6-7 NIV). How awesome! I can know who God is by looking at Jesus! So whatever Jesus said about relationships was the advice I wanted to follow. While this guy I'd just met might not be someone I'd date for long, I didn't care. Deep inside I felt this first date was just was the beginning of a wellspring of blessings and my time in the arid wasteland, with no prospects in sight, was coming to an end; leading me to a refreshing oasis.

My roommate and I had a great time touring Upstate New York in early July. One evening, we had dinner with several of my high school girlfriends; one who wanted to fix me up with a close friend of hers. He lived in Virginia about three hours from Raleigh. He was divorced without children, but wanted to remarry and have a family. She didn't know much about the church he attended, but said he wanted to meet a church-going woman too. She asked if she could give him my phone number and let us decide the next course of action. That was fine with me; I appreciated her thinking of me. Dating had become a great adventure again, and I considered this all practice until God revealed the right man to me.

Shortly after I returned from Syracuse her friend from Virginia called me. We had a great conversation, and the initial connection between us was positive, so we decided to meet for lunch in Rocky Mount, North Carolina about half-way for each of us. When I walked into the restaurant, and introduced myself, with a wide-eyed look he said, "Wow, you're half my size!" He was a handsome man over six feet tall and weighed 230 pounds, by his own admission. His comments about my appearance were shockingly honest; I think I looked better than he expected which made me laugh. More than once he exclaimed he just couldn't believe I'd never been married.

We covered the usual first-date topics of work, family, and places we'd lived; then he brought up the subject of faith. He said he believed in Jesus and had heard the "born again message", as he called it, from his best friend who was Baptist. However, he'd dismissed the message believing Jesus was one way, but not the only way to gain entrance into heaven. His best friend expressed concern about his salvation because of his beliefs, but he told his friend, "Don't worry I've got it covered." He said Jesus was one of many great teachers, and other beliefs were just as valid.

A bit disappointed at this juncture, I didn't let him know; I wasn't sure what to say. I liked him, and wanted to know

me a great guy (although He could), but to do my best to honor Him with my body. I often referred to 1 Corinthians 6:19-20 (NIV) to keep me on track: "Do you not know that your body is a temple of the Holy Spirit who is in you, whom you have received from God? You are not your own; you were bought at a price. Therefore, honor God with your body." I prayed for the Holy Spirit to strengthen me, and keep me from neglecting the good health I'd received. While I was responsible for doing my part to take care of myself, Jesus would take care of the rest; causing a man to fall perfectly in love with me (and I with him) regardless of our flaws.

For the very first time, I appreciated my body just as it was; marveling at the way it was healing. Prior to my surgery I'd been so critical of myself; focusing primarily on my short-comings. Scars no longer represented flaws to me, but were evidence of survival, and reminders of restoration. At last the stronghold was broken, and I was free from the curse of perfectionism! Naturally, I still wanted to look attractive, but I was no longer obsessed and worried my physique wasn't appealing enough to men. Inside and out I was filled with a healthy vibrancy. As my love and knowledge of Jesus were growing in sync, I felt burdens being lifted from me like never before. Barriers between me and God were breaking down, and bridges were built that connected me to God's love and grace. I'd crossed the great divide from spiritual death into abundant life, and wasted no time looking over my shoulder to my former ways.

Later that summer, I began praying for Jesus to bless the guys I'd loved and lost to other women. As I prayed for blessings for my former boyfriends, my thinking started to shift. I no longer dwelled on why these relationships had

n't have the answer, perhaps God didn't want
he reason, or was teaching me to trust in His
ny faith would increase. I had learned about
praying for those who'd hurt me in Job 42:10 (NIV): "After
Job prayed for his friends, the Lord made him prosperous
again and gave him twice as much as he had before." Putting this into practice, I prayed their marriages would be
strong and happy; that God would watch over them. This
didn't come naturally, but with repetition it eventually felt
good to pray for someone else to be blessed, no matter how
they'd treated me. Old wounds were healing; I couldn't
stay angry while praying for their welfare!

When it came to dating, I'd made some very bad choices
before. I often used the excuse for doing things I knew
were sinful stating, "Well if God doesn't like what I'm doing then He's going to have to change me." Or, "I know I
shouldn't be involved with this man, but if God doesn't approve then why did we meet?" My words were a clear reflection that my heart was not open to God doing any kind
of transformation in me. I was not a willing participant in
Christ's redemptive work in my life, and didn't want to assume responsibility for the outcome of my choices. It was
easier for me to believe that everything that happened to me
was fate. In other words, it wasn't my fault. I was just a
victim of my circumstances; therefore it was up to God to
change me.

Sometimes I felt so ashamed looking back at my sins, but it
also caused me to praise God for forgiveness. Now that I
was spiritually born again I didn't want to sin, or do anything outside of His perfect will. I wanted to be obedient to
His calling for my life. My strength and joy would come
from Jesus; I wasn't going to let my circumstances rule

over my emotions anymore. There was nothing God and I couldn't overcome together! What a satisfying time this was having my hunger fed through Bible study, mentoring, and church participation. Daily I thanked God for being unemployed; allowing me more healing time, and communion with Him. Sometimes I still wondered if He was preparing me for missionary work. *Since many jobs and men had been stripped away from me, perhaps God was equipping me for a solo life abroad serving Him?* Funny thing was, once more my idea of God's plan for my life was different from His.

Chapter 18
The Mission Field Defined

"Then I head the voice of the Lord saying, "Whom shall I send? And who will go for us?" And I said, "Here am I, send me (Isaiah 6:8 NIV)!"

The first week of August, I was airborne en route to Colorado and New Mexico for a seven-day visit. Hopeful a job was somewhere on the horizon, I decided to take a road-trip prior to working again. I'd had occasional interviews, but no offers yet. Employers were taking much longer to make a decision, so the timing was good to head out west. My first stop was the home of my cousin, and her family, in Colorado Springs. After we took in the sights in various regions of Colorado, I rented a car and drove to see my former co-worker living in Albuquerque. She was a mother now, and I was looking forward to meeting my four-month-old godson for the first time.

Driving alone from Colorado Springs to Albuquerque was a bit of a stretch for me considering I didn't own a cell phone, and had never driven that route before. Even so, it was exhilarating to be brave. There was something very liberating about driving solo in parts of those states I hadn't seen until now. While taking in the varied landscape around me, I reflected on all the changes I'd been through in recent months. I was still in amazement that my attitude about my life (especially the hardships and trials) had been completely overhauled by God's grace. Quietly, I thanked Jesus as I drove on in excitement towards my destination in New Mexico.

Visiting my friend in Albuquerque was very special. Seeing her as a mother; holding the baby she'd prayed and longed for, was so tender. All I could do was rejoice in her happiness. She'd been so helpful during my research for a cure for my fibroids. What a gift to visit with her, and talk about how God blessed us both in different ways this past spring. Walking around Santa Fe, with her son in tow, it felt as if the world was as it should be. There was so much peace in both our lives, and I was so glad I was back in New Mexico again. The diverse beauty of that region always causes me to marvel at God's creative genius. Forget Mother Nature-- thank you Father God!

Upon my return to Raleigh, I heard from the guy in Virginia and we set up our second date. As we drove to a party a friend of mine was hosting, the topic of our beliefs came up. He typically started these conversations whenever we spoke, so I suspected he was curious about my faith. *Perhaps he was searching for answers and more open to hearing the Gospel than I'd immediately thought? I'm glad I didn't dismiss him on our first date.* But my hope quickly faded when he voiced his opinion that there were ma ligions that had good practices and asked, "So how ﹍uid they all be wrong and following Jesus Christ be the only right way?" He felt he was a good person overall, and God would welcome him into heaven because only really bad people went to hell.

Without hesitation, words sprang forth from my mouth that I never anticipated saying. Playing the role of instigator I asked, "If there are other ways to gain access into heaven besides belief in what Jesus did on the cross for our sins, then what was the point of his death?" *Wow! Where did that come from? It must be the Holy Spirit, I'm not that profound.* Instantly, our lively conversation ended rendering us speechless for the rest of the drive. Behind our happy party faces, we both sensed this was ill-fated. I didn't want to ignore God's instructions and date a guy who was not saved, or seeking a relationship with Jesus. Like subjecting a positive force to a negative one, the negative will always deplete the positive. I'd read about King Saul in 1 Samuel 15 who offered sacrifices to God while building palaces and gardens for his unbelieving wives to worship their gods. Disobedient to God's command when he married pagan women; his sacrifices were attempts to make atonement for his sin. God was not pleased with Saul's sacrifices; they did not cleanse him from his dismal of the Lord's command. Saul's footsteps were not ones I wanted to walk in.

Never claiming to have attained mature wisdom in God's ways this much I knew, I wanted my relationship with a man to have His blessing and this one didn't. We were unequally yoked. It wasn't my responsibility to save this man, or anyone else in my path. All I could do was plant seeds of

God's truth and pray they'd take root. The rest was up to the Holy Spirit. As he graciously said good-bye, inviting me to visit him anytime in Virginia, I thanked him but offered no response. We parted ways peacefully and painlessly. No harsh words were spoken; no debates trying to convince each other which one was right in our beliefs. It was better this way.

For all I knew, our meeting might have been a test of my faith. *Did I honestly trust the Father's ability to bring me a God-fearing husband, or would I panic and settle for an appealing but unbelieving man?* Whether or not my purpose was to stimulate his mind to examine his beliefs, I'll never know. Regardless, I wasn't going to expend enormous amounts of energy trying to decipher why I had stories galore to share, but no companion as my match. Reviewing the details of these dates with my mentor, she confirmed God wasn't torturing me. Actually, He was training me to trust Him for greater things. Consequently, I was discovering joy and satisfaction in fellowshipping with Jesus. *Suppose I never marry. Is God enough for me?* Comforted by His love even in my questioning, it wasn't a burden to obey Him. Whenever I believed I'd received an answer to a prayer, I searched the Bible for clarity instead of reacting based on my intuition. Just because something felt right didn't mean it necessarily was. Emotions had deceived me before. Now I knew they were no substitute for God's Word.

Romans 12:1-2 (NIV) was a Scripture we reviewed often in our summer Bible study, "Therefore, I urge you brothers in view of God's mercy, to offer your bodies as living sacrifices, holy and pleasing to God—this is your spiritual act of worship. Do not conform any longer to the pattern of this

world, but be transformed by the renewing of your mind. Then you will be able to test and approve what God's will is—His good, pleasing and perfect will." As I meditated on these words, I realized God would educate me in His ways so I could discern which path was to be taken. Godly wisdom could be mine! So when family and friends asked why this latest love interest didn't last, I said, "It was because of differences in our faith." Some made no comment while others responded, "Well, I don't think it matters what you believe as long as you believe in something, and you're sincere about it." All I could think of is that sincerity in one's beliefs is not validation of divine truth, and if not for God's grace in my life I would still be sincerely lost.

As Labor Day approached, I was still looking for work along with every technical recruiter I knew. Sometimes it looked like an opportunity was opening up; then the door would shut again. While it had been wonderful having the last four months off to recover from surgery, I never completely relaxed because I was always looking for work. My savings had dwindled, but if I had to I could make it last until the end of the year. I thanked God for the monetary blessing He'd provided previously when my income was high, and was hopeful financial restoration was coming soon. No longer resentful as I'd been in years past when trials came my way, this time I thought, *What makes me so special that I think I'm immune to hard times? People have been through worse than this. If I just hang in there, and keep applying, the right job will surface. God is teaching me patience, persistence and perseverance through hardship. This is happening for my good, and I will be a person of greater character because of it.* God was on my side, and I was in His perfect will exactly where I was.

In the days that followed, I revisited the thought that perhaps the reason I wasn't finding work, or meeting the right man, was because I was going to be serving God as a single woman in missions. Until now I'd kept these thoughts private, knowing being public about them might bring them into reality. On the one hand, it was frightening to entertain leaving the comfort of familiar surroundings and go wherever the Lord led me. On the other hand, I knew if this was His purpose for my life He'd confirm it, and equip me to be a missionary. My mentor agreed to pray with me that I would have clarity on what my path was. She knew I still hoped to be married, but said the most fulfilling life I could ever lead would be the one God had designed for me.

The morning of September 11th began in typical form as I checked my email messages. Having recently interviewed with a pharmaceutical company one-hour away, I was hoping for an update from them. A close friend, and manager there, had recommended me for a three-month contract on his team. There was mutual interest after my phone interview, but no decision yet. Glancing through my inbox, a note appeared from our Sunday school class worship leader. He often sent out devotionals, but this one was a prayer request. His simple message read, "Folks, let's pray for the people and events in New York City and DC today." I sent a reply asking, "Please pardon my ignorance, I didn't watch the morning news. What happened?"

He responded with the news that two planes had flown into the Twin Towers in New York City, and one hit the Pentagon. I was shocked and immediately turned on the television. What a horrible sight! After watching the towers crash down to the ground, I was stunned and scared. No one knew if more attacks were forthcoming. I called everyone in my family to tell them I loved them, and eventually reached one of my girlfriends who worked near the Twin Towers. She was wandering around the New York City streets in shock, but she was okay. I was relieved to hear her voice, but so upset for all those people who lost loved ones.

As the day wore on, I started to believe this catastrophic event would worsen the already fragile American economy; forcing many into a perilous financial state. I was sure this was the end of working in corporate America for me. But on September 12th I received a call from the human resources representative of the pharmaceutical company offering me the contract job I'd interviewed for. My friend would be my boss. *Who could have imagined this?* In the middle of a terrible national tragedy God blessed me with a job. The hourly rate was excellent, and there was a possibility they'd extend the contract beyond December. Accepting the offer, I started on September 18th, amazed I'd be recruiting again when there were so few jobs in my field. For now, the office and everyday life was going to be my mission field; not living in a tent in another country.

That same week, a married couple from church introduced me to a guy who owned a carpet cleaning franchise. He was a Christian in his early 40's divorced without children, but wanted to remarry and have kids. They thought we'd be a good match. About a week later, he called as I walked in the door from work; asking if he could pick me up that night. Even though it was a last minute date I accepted the invitation. The next few hours weren't really what I expected for a first date. We didn't go anywhere to sit and talk. Instead, we drove around in his car while he complained about his employees, and the challenges of owning a franchise. He asked my opinion on dealing with some of the employees; assuming I'd have some insight as a recruiter. I explained employee relations were handled by human resources professionals, not recruiters, but offered some common sense suggestions about talking with the employees, and putting goals and expectations in writing for them.

Unfortunately, his personal life was just as chaotic as his business. He owned a house; renting one of the bedrooms to another man. He liked the guy, but was not happy his girlfriend often spent the night there. When asked if he'd ever spoken with his roommate about this, he couldn't seem to give me a clear answer. While he wasn't a bad looking guy, and we shared the same beliefs, I wasn't sure I could handle his complaining, and lack of good communication skills. Rather than jump to conclusions, I accepted another opportunity to go out with him. *Perhaps this was a fluke and he was just having a bad day.* I'd dated enough to know that not every first date went smoothly, and wanted to remain open to see what God revealed as I prayed for discernment.

A few days later, his phone call came in similar fashion to the first one. It was early in the evening; he was driving around, and wanted to meet somewhere for dessert. I was beginning to wonder if this was a pattern. No commitments, no advance plans, just a last minute phone call as if I were a passing thought in his day, but not really all that important. I declined that night, but agreed on a more convenient day a week later. He promised he'd call me to confirm. I wasn't feeling very optimistic about this guy, but since he committed to a future day and time, I'd give him another chance.

Although our three-month commitment was completed, my mentor and I decided to continue our meetings. Sometimes in our gatherings I'd cry. As entertaining as it was to have lots of funny stories to share about the men in my life, I was puzzled that none were my chosen mate. But my tears ended as she sited Scriptures that proved God could be trusted, and Christ-likeness is developed through suffering. Conversations with my mentor helped me see the value in being born again while single. God wanted my undivided attention right now. When I'm ready to meet my husband He wouldn't delay in presenting him. As I continued praying for my future spouse, and that I'd be a good wife, my hope increased. I knew however God answered my prayers it would be special. "Every good and perfect gift is from above, coming down from the Father of the heavenly lights, who does not change like shifting shadows" (James 1:17 NIV). Instead of wondering why we hadn't met, I got excited about what God was doing behind the scenes. I felt a surprise coming my way, and that is was going to be really good.

Chapter 19
Walking on a Bridge

"For I am going to do something in your days that you would not believe, even it you were told" (Habakkuk 1:5 NIV).

Monday, October 15th was a warm sunny day. Home from work, I quickly changed clothes so I could walk around Lake Lynn adjoining my apartment complex. I was in a hurry to get some exercise, eat dinner, and shower before going to church for Bible study. Many people were walking on that summer-like evening in early autumn, as I quickly passed them by. Happy in my own little world, I was thankful to be feeling stronger physically and emotionally. In my head, I was silently praising God for all the blessings I had in my life—my job, health, family and friends, and most of all my relationship with His Son. I was completely engulfed in my own thoughts as I briskly walked along the lakeside path when something happened.

As my feet sprang off the pavement I felt as light as a feather; softly landing on one of the wooden bridges cascading over the water. Suddenly, my wistful state was jolted by a man walking towards me happily exclaiming, "Hey, there she is!" *Was he talking to me? Had I met him before somewhere? His voice sounded familiar like an old friend saying, "Hello."* Thoughts flashed through my head as fast as lightning as he held out his hand with a big smile saying, "Hi, I'm Jon." Locked in a handshake I replied, "I'm Mary." Proceeding to confess he'd noticed me in worship services, he admitted sporadic attendance. Jon worked a rotating shift in the power marketing group of a local utility company. Previously involved in the same Sunday school class and Wednesday night singles gathering we possibly crossed paths, but I didn't recognize him. Thinking now how friendly this tall, dark and handsome man was; I wondered how I'd overlooked him before.

Standing on that bridge, oblivious to all around us, we exchanged general information. Jon lived across the street in a condo and, like me, had been walking this lakeside trail for two years. *Incredible! We'd probably passed each other dozens of times. Wonder why he stopped me in my tracks today?* He seemed very interested, as if he was going to ask me out, as he eagerly kept our conversation going. However, seconds later he brought closure by saying, "Well, since we attend many of the same singles functions I guess I'll see you at church sometime." *Okay, false alarm; maybe he's not interested in dating me. Oh well, nice to have met him anyway.* Exchanging good-byes as we walked off in opposite directions, I laughed to myself over thoughts of God extending my summer of love into the fall. What fun this was going to be!

Two days later, I was walking my usual fast and focused pace around Lake Lynn when thoughts of Jon popped into my head. Silently, I began conversing with God. *You know Lord, there's something different about that man. He seems really nice. If you want us to spend time together, you're going to have to do something because we don't have each other's contact information. Since Jon works a rotating shift, who knows when we'll see each other again? It's up to you.* Wrapping up my internal dialog with God, I noticed a man walking in front of me, but didn't recognize him. Just as I started to pass him on the left he said, "Hi Mary." It was Jon! *That was the quickest answer to prayer I'd ever received!*

How embarrassing to be caught off guard especially when he said, "You seemed like you were deep in thought." *Quick, Mary, offer a clever response!* The best I could conjure up was that I was thinking about work. Thankfully, he accepted my statement without asking for specifics! We walked beside each other eventually reaching the trailhead where I'd take the path to my apartment. Before we parted, Jon asked if he could call me to walk again with him sometime. Accepting his invitation, I said my last name was Singer and my number was listed. Sharing his was Wick and his number was listed too, he smiled as he turned to walk away. Floating on air as I headed home, I wondered when I'd hear from him; hoping he wouldn't tarry.

That night at the gathering, I told my girlfriends I met a handsome guy from our church walking around Lake Lynn, and he asked if he could call me! One girlfriend told me not to get too excited, "You've met a lot of men lately. But if this one doesn't work out, it just means you're one step closer to the right one." I agreed with her. These last few months, as the Lord built up my faith and trust in Him, my confidence had grown in His provision too. I was more at peace and happier than ever before. My desires had changed from petitioning God to grant me all that I wanted for my life, to having my life be all that He desired it to be. Whatever His perfect will was for me that is where I wanted to dwell.

The next day, I was pleasantly surprised when I came home from work to Jon's message on my answering machine. He asked if I wanted to go for a walk around the lake that night, leaving his cell and home phone numbers. Funny how our brain sometimes hears only what it wants to hear, and translates the original message into something completely different. As I continued listening to his message I thought he said, "Don't be surprised when you call my home number if my dog answers the phone." Laughing as I pondered how strange that was, I quickly realized he'd said his daughter; not his dog!

With a loud thud my daydream crashed into reality; smashing it into pieces. *Sigh, what a short lifespan.* Whenever I'd prayed for a husband, I pictured one who wanted to be a father; not someone who already was one. This news made me hesitant; unsure how close to Jon I wanted to get. Life would be less complicated without an ex-wife and child in the picture. Resisting the temptation to dismiss him as "not my type", I silenced my inner critic. I didn't know Jon, or his situation. *Perhaps he's a widower?* The fact that he'd traveled a road I'd yet to see exposed my prejudice, and wrong point of view. Evidently, God wanted us to spend time together given He'd answered my prayer with a second meeting of Jon at the lake. But that didn't mean we were going to get serious. Committing this to prayer, I asked God to guide me; alerting me to any red flags that were heaven's signals to stop. Trusting Jesus, I forged ahead.

Returning Jon's call, we agreed to meet on the trail below my apartment. As we walked the two-and-one-half mile loop around Lake Lynn, we talked about our backgrounds, families, and the usual small-talk people exchange when trying to gain insight into the other. When he mentioned being divorced with three daughters in college; the youngest were twins who lived with him, my mind became a careening vessel. *Run, Mary! He's got three kids, not one, and an ex-wife! How will you ever handle all these women clamoring for his attention? This can't be good.* But I didn't run. I kept walking; telling myself to relax. Jon was such a kind soul, and I liked listening to him. Maybe he's not for me and there's another reason we met. In any case, I wanted to proceed with caution; not making any false judgments.

Jon asked me if I'd ever been married, or had children. When I responded, "No, but I'd like to be", he thought there must be something wrong with me. He theorized I was crazy, and any moment the evidence would prove him right. Like me, he wanted to run but didn't. Obviously, neither of us shared these fears and thoughts with each other that first walking date. They were mentioned in later conversations. As we finished walking, Jon said he'd like to spend more time getting to know me. I looked forward to that and told him to call whenever he was available. He was working the weekend shift; I was bound for Sunset Beach, North Carolina and a singles retreat with the church. While I was disappointed that dating a man with a pre-existing family wasn't what I'd prayed for, I knew God had a reason for it all, and in time that would be revealed.

The following week, the guy who owned his own carpet cleaning franchise left a message on my voice mail. A few days earlier he'd cancelled our planned date at the last minute. Now he was calling just as he always had saying he'd be in my area, and wondered if I wanted to get together with him that night. It was clear this man wasn't for me; so I never saw him again. He wasn't dependable, and I'd grown tired of phone calls at the end of the day asking if I could do something right then and there. I thanked my friends for fixing us up, but let them know I wasn't interested in him. I'd met a new guy I was spending more time with.

One day a close friend called asking for a favor. She was going for her final bridal gown fitting and asked if I could come with her. Her matron-of-honor was her sister who lived in Tennessee, and she didn't have anyone else who was available that evening. Meeting her after work in the bridal shop, my mind began to wander as I knelt down and straightened the hem of her dress, *"Oh Lord, will I ever be the bride?"* She was an inspiration to me. It was her first marriage and she was only two months older than me. We'd met through the local ski and outing club, and had made a lot of good memories together. Her husband-to-be was also a club member, so all of our friends would be going to their wedding. She looked beautiful and even as I wondered if it would ever by my turn, I was excited it was hers.

At her wedding I shared with friends the story of meeting Jon a few weeks earlier. Even though this had just happened, they felt good things were in store for me. I had to agree with them. Somehow I knew good things were in my future with or without Jon. In the past, I'd always pleaded with God to make things work in my favor when I met a man I liked. This time I prayed for His guidance, and asked Him to help me listen to what He was saying to me. I was hopeful and expectant as I waited to see what He'd bring forth in my life, promising to rejoice no matter what it was. Since He'd brought Jon to me, I asked Jesus to remove my fears and prejudices about dating a divorced father, and to quicken our hearts for each other. Lastly, I prayed we'd both have godly wisdom to know if we were to continue or stop dating. This time dating would be different for me, or at least that is what I'd hoped.

Chapter 20
Favor with God and a Man

"Ah, Sovereign Lord, you have made the heavens and the earth by your great power and out stretched arm. Nothing is too hard for you" (Jeremiah 32:17 NIV).

As October rolled into November, Jon called whenever he wasn't working to see if we could get together. We attended the singles gathering and Sunday school together; discovering we knew some of the same people. It's funny how our paths probably crossed before the day we met walking around Lake Lynn, but God wasn't ready to lift the blinds until then. One evening, Jon appeared nervous as we walked around the lake. He asked me to sit down on a wooden bench right near the bridge where we'd met. *Oh no, here it comes. That speech about how I deserve someone better because he doesn't want to remarry or have more children. If that's what he's about to tell me, I'd rather he get it over with now than be deceptive and keep on dating me.*

Tentatively sitting beside him, Jon caught me off guard revealing he didn't want to play the field. While unsure if I was the woman he would marry one day, eventually he wanted to remarry and was dating with that purpose in mind. Jon believed we were mutually interested in each other, but he'd been hood-winked before. If I was a gunslinger, biding my time until a better cowboy rode into town, he wanted no part of my scheme. He preferred to date me to see if we had lasting potential. However, if my goal differed he wanted to make a clean getaway before becoming my next casualty.

Is he for real? What a concept—a guy who doesn't want to compare me to every other woman out there, but is serious about getting to know me! Never in my dating experience had a man broached the topic of marriage this early; asking me to state my honest intentions. Without pausing, I agreed with Jon. While I didn't know if he was the man I'd marry either, I enjoyed being around him, and wanted to date him exclusively. Knowing how hard it must have been to expose his desires to me, I thanked him; congratulating him on a job well done. He laughed admitting he was nervous beforehand, but felt better now that we'd talked. As we strolled around the lake that cool evening, I felt so peaceful beside Jon. He'd set a positive tone by removing any doubt of his intentions; I found safety in his words. This was a good man; one I was really happy I was going to spend more time with.

Attending the singles gathering together always prompted great discussions afterwards. One Wednesday night the pastor preached on remarriage according to God's Word. It was no coincidence we were about to study this same topic in Sunday school. Clearly, the Lord was opening up a door for conversations between Jon and me. Although it was such a delicate area to navigate, I wanted to understand why Jon was divorced. Knowing all the details wasn't necessary, but there were some things I needed to be educated on. If Jon was part of a harsh situation, filled with lots of conflict, I wanted nothing to do with it.

As we sat in his truck that evening, he was willing to share limited information. We both agreed some basic facts were important to discuss now, but in the interest of respect and privacy we wouldn't share this information with others. Jon said as we grew closer he'd reveal more about his divorce to me, but thought it was too early to share all of our sad stories involving past relationships. He was afraid it might do us more harm than good. Jon wasn't trying to be dishonest, but to talk about our previous relationships slowly, delicately, and in its proper time. I was very impressed that he didn't speak with bitterness when he talked about his ex-wife. He accepted responsibility for his role in the divorce, and had been counseled by the church. Seems we'd both been on a path of healing and forgiveness over the last few years; long before we met.

Seeking to establish some boundaries in our relationship, Jon took the lead that night, and introduced another topic for discussion. He said we shouldn't sleep together unless we are married to each other. He wouldn't stay late at my apartment or ever overnight, nor would I stay at his condo. We'd take no vacations alone together. If we traveled together they would be chaperoned events like church retreats, or family visits. Jon said he didn't want to ever give anyone a reason to look at me in a bad light, or for me to feel shame. If he spent the night with me, even if we didn't sleep together, people wouldn't believe us. Our actions would lead them to think otherwise, and draw different conclusions, thus damaging our witness for purity before marriage.

How wonderful to hear those words! No man had ever respected me so much that he was concerned about my reputation. I felt so valued by Jon, and in complete agreement I added that I didn't think we should kiss passionately for a long time. There was no specific timeline in my mind, but I knew if we started kissing I'd get too emotionally attached to him; risking my tendency to be blinded by my emotions. So many times I'd mistaken attraction for love. Loving someone can include physical attraction, or attraction can simply be lust. It's a conscious choice to love another, and it starts with first responding to Jesus' love for us. "We love because He first loved us" (I John 4:19 NIV). We can't always control who we are attracted to, but we can choose who we love, and how we love. Jon agreed saying we'd greet each other with a quick hug; say good night the same way, but no kissing for now.

As the conversation came to a close, he walked me to my door before driving home. What a great night! How refreshing to hear Jon wanted to spend time getting to know who I was on the inside—what my thoughts and feelings were; what my goals and dreams were, as well as my values. This was starting out to be the most logical relationship I'd ever had. I wondered if he would be romantic at all, but I wasn't looking for that side of him so early in our courtship. This was a whole new experience for me, dating according to God's instructions, and I was about to learn what true romance really is.

As we moved through November, our walking dates turned into more varied ones like going to a play, bike riding, dinner, and watching a meteor shower one morning with several other onlookers. Before one of our dates Jon introduced me to his twin daughters. His oldest daughter attended college in Long Beach, California, and lived with her mother. The twins had come to live with Jon, and attend a local community college. Jon believed it was important we spend time with our families and friends; observing how we interacted with people we'd known for years. While it was too soon to be taking trips to meet my family in New York, and the rest of his in Montana and California, we'd start with our North Carolina connections.

The more time we spent together, the more I liked being with Jon. He was a great conversationalist, good listener and very caring man. He took the lead in our relationship in every area, and this was something I thoroughly relished. I felt so safe with Jon knowing he was truly interested in learning about me, and wanted to build trust between us. One of his best suggestions was that we read about healthy relationships together. I'd never read a book with any guy on topics that would strengthened our dating relationship. What a great idea! Jon believed healthy and thriving relationships were consciously created; not a product of happenstance. We can have what we want in our relationship, and it can be good or bad depending on our choices.

We both wanted to make wise choices, and simultaneously pledged we'd always strive to be edifying to each other; speaking positively about the other person, especially in public. If I had a problem with anything Jon was doing (or not doing) he wanted me to let him know in a loving and private way; not gossip about his faults with my girlfriends, or seek their advice on how to fix him. Attending Providence Baptist Church was very important to him, and he didn't want to have to leave the church if we broke up because people were upset with him. I understood, and completely supported, everything Jon said on this subject. This was the same way I wanted to be treated by him.

Right from the start, Jon and I made it a priority to not allow negative comments to be part of our language of relating to each other. We directed our energy toward looking for the best qualities in each other, and chose words that would foster the growth of good behavior. We weren't blinding ourselves to any potential harmful traits by concentrating on positive attributes, because we continually asked God to reveal to us what was truth and what was a façade. When something bothered us, we talked about it in a civil way, without attacking each other. This way of communicating allowed us the freedom to be honest, without fear of reproach. Even though everything was going smoothly, I was still hesitant about the long-term view. If I married Jon, I'd have to blend into a pre-existing family, and even under the best of circumstances, that thought scared me. However, this was another reason for me to keep going to Jesus in prayer for wisdom; letting Him, not my emotions, decide the course I should take. As long as I kept an open-mind, looked for Him to answer me, and obeyed God's direction, I had no reason to fear.

Jon was scared too. By now, he was able to admit he wondered if something dark was going to surface; then he'd understand why I'd never married. *How strange it was for me to be thought of as abnormal because I wasn't divorced.* I suppose the case could've been made that at least someone wanted me once, even if the marriage didn't last. But for now, Jon had to do his own seeking to find out what God was revealing to him about me. It wasn't my responsibility to convince Jon I was worthy to be his wife. As he prayed for discernment, Jesus would tell him what to do. We were both committed to God's answer no matter what it was because we knew God was for us; not against us. He would protect us in our obedience to His commands.

On chilly afternoons, we'd sit fireside, alternating turns reading a chapter of a book out loud to each other; pausing to discuss what we read. I found it very romantic to listen to Jon read to me. It was so comforting, like being a little girl again, cherished in his presence. We'd discuss things like: "How do you feel about being a grandparent? What do you envision for your future? What are your financial priorities? Have you been saving for retirement? What are some of the mistakes you've made in life; what did you learn from them? How did you come to know Jesus as your Lord and Savior? What is most important to you? Do you want children and if so, how many?" As reassuring as talking about these important topics was, I didn't trust Jon's answers as the final authority to base my decision on whether or not we'd marry one day. Any of us can give a clever answer to what we think the other person wants to hear. We'd both been fooled before. In time, our actions would either validate or negate our words; so we proceeded forward with our eyes and ears open.

In December, I went skiing with friends in Steamboat Springs, Colorado. We participated in a one-week ski clinic perfecting our skills while having a blast! Jon saw me off at the Raleigh-Durham airport, and greeted me upon my return. I missed being away from him but our reunion didn't last for long. Shortly thereafter, he left for a business trip in

Las Vegas for a few days. At the same time, I said farewell to my Turkish roommate who moved out mid-month. She wanted to live alone for the first time in her life. We'd spent over two years together, and shared a lot. I knew we'd keep in touch, and was glad she was doing something she felt was important.

Since I had enough money to cover her share of the rent for awhile, I decided to live alone too. Renewing my lease until June 2002, I would revisit the subject of a roommate if living solo was too expensive. Now that I'd be alone, I had to be strong and not create a tempting atmosphere for Jon. We talked about this; the rules were still the same—no sleeping over, no late nights, and no sex. This would take prayer and discipline, but I knew we'd keep our promise if we stayed committed together.

Christmas was celebrated with my family in Syracuse while Jon stayed in Raleigh and worked. He picked me up at the airport when I returned on December 30th and we made plans for our New Years Eve celebration. We rang in the New Year by going to three different house parties. Our midnight kiss was a simple one, and when Jon dropped me off around 1 AM, we were looking forward to hiking on New Years day in the state park up the street. After a very fun evening, I crawled into my cozy bed with a smile on my face, and had happy dreams.

On January 2nd, we attended the gathering as a light snow began falling. Two hours later, on the way home, the pace accelerated and the snow began accumulating quickly. Not ready to end the evening, I asked Jon if he wanted to walk around Lake Lynn, and was thrilled when he said yes. *Such bliss to know this man was as crazy as me about going out*

142

in a snow storm! He went home to change his clothes, and I did the same. When he returned to my apartment, we were all bundled up as we headed out into the elements, with my camera tucked safely in my coat pocket.

What a beautiful and romantic winter night for a walk as the snow quietly fell all around us. Jon said the snowflakes made me look pretty as they landed on my eye lashes. I was glad we decided to go for this spontaneous walk together, giving us another opportunity to talk, and reflect on the day. There were a few lights on around the lake and they were enough to guide our footsteps. We only saw one other couple strolling like us, and they had their camera too! We took photos of each other then Jon walked me home; promising he'd call in the morning. He already had the week off, but we had a feeling I wouldn't be working either if the snow continued throughout the night.

Sure enough, the next day I was snowed in. We'd received 15 inches of glorious snow, turning the landscape into a picturesque winter wonderland! Jon came over to help me shovel, and paused to build a snowman. We walked around the lake, and saw people sledding on whatever they could find—cardboard boxes, plastic sleds; even an old mattress! We made dinner at my apartment, and watched a movie fireside while the multi-colored Christmas tree lights glowed against the snow outside. Jon continued to be a gentleman, and I found our time together bringing us closer as we talked, laughed and shared our hearts. There was so much more to learn, and I wanted to keep exploring.

Chapter 21
The Start of Many Firsts

"The Lord blessed the latter part of Job's life more than the first" (Job 42:12 NIV).

B y mid-January our hearts entered the magical land of deep infatuation where reality doesn't take up residence. However, rather than let our emotions cloud our reason, we decided to talk to our singles pastor. Jon took the initiative to schedule the appointment, explaining we wanted to explore his remarriage possibilities. Although nervous, we wanted to seek godly counsel on this, and not make our own assumptions. One Sunday afternoon, we met in the pastor's office for a two-hour counseling session. During that meeting two things left a firm impression on me. The first was Jon's willing attitude to be transparent and respectful to his former wife regarding their divorce, and his comment to the pastor that he wasn't looking for a technical "out clause". He wanted to know, according to

God's Word, if he could remarry. The second was the pastor and how he responded by looking at what the Bible said; showing us the Scriptures. He wasn't answering our questions based on his own opinion, but on what he believed God says about divorce and remarriage.

As with any emotional topic, there were ups and downs in the conversation. I listened more than I talked since Jon had to answer the questions. At times, I was overcome with fear thinking Jon wasn't eligible to be remarried in our church, and how hard it would be to break up. But more than get married, I wanted to be obedient to God's Word, and His will. *It's in the Lord's hands, and He knows best.* By the end of the meeting, we had the pastor's assurance that Jon was eligible to remarry so we could continue dating. What a relief it was to know that information now! We were both exhausted as we left his office, but glad we went through the process together.

That experience led us into deeper conversations involving the subject of children. Jon appeared to be mulling the idea over these last few months. Previously, he said 90% of him didn't want more children, but the other 10% was open. As we talked that night, I told him about the myomectomy surgery I'd had nine months earlier, and the obstacles I'd faced in hopes of having a child. Even though I was 43, and Jon was 47, I still wanted to have a baby if we got married. Although he was very sympathetic, he admitted he wasn't sure if he really wanted more children. Even if he did, it would require him having an expensive surgery. Disappointed by his words, I hid my sadness from Jon that night, unable to adequately express my feelings. He went home thinking everything was fine, but by the next day reality set in. I felt he'd mislead me; that he hadn't been clear with me before. He'd given me the impression he was open to having more children, even if it was with only a 10% certainty. Until now, I was unaware he'd be the one needing surgery if we were to be parents together. This was not the news I wanted to hear.

For two days, I refused responding to Jon's calls and emails. My mind was filled with doubt as voices from past conversations with friends visited me now. "Since God spared your uterus He must plan to give you a baby." All these months I'd believed that too. *Father, how could you allow me to keep the ability to bear children but give me a man who can't? Why is this dream threatened again? What more do I need to sacrifice?* Aware this line of questioning could sink me into a dark abyss of indignation; I had to stop the downward spiral. Not everything in life needed to revolve around my wishes. There were other people to consider. Arising from my selfish-state, I answered Jon's pleas; agreeing to meet with our singles pastor before this became a wedge between us.

As we stated our dilemma for the pastor, he interjected his thoughts at the end of our presentation. Weighing the facts, he concluded the choice was mine to make. His words came on the heels of Jon's admission that while he didn't want to squelch my dream of motherhood, he couldn't promise to fulfill it. The pastor said I had to decide if having a baby was more important than having Jon. *How unfair!* Although it was unintentional on their part, I felt ganged up on; angry this was all on my conscience. Yet a part of me knew some kind of decision had to be made. Distraught and unable to speak what my heart felt, Jon acquiesced somewhat by offering to explore all possibilities further. So as not to raise my expectations, he cautioned he was still unsure about adding additional children to his life. Thanking the pastor for his insight, we quietly exited his office knowing there was more work ahead of us.

Back home I cried and prayed to God for an answer, and a resolution to this constant source of torment. My mentor prayed with me for God's will. Within a few days, I felt the Lord asking me to trust Him on this subject, and to keep going forward with Jon. "Have I not commanded you? Be strong and courageous. Do not be terrified; do not be discouraged for the Lord your God will be with you wherever you go" (Joshua 1:9 NIV). So I told Jon I didn't want to break up with him, but I wasn't completely ready to give up on children, and would consider adoption. We both agreed to talk about this again, and pray for the Lord to change our hearts so we'd be in line with His plans. After exchanging apologies we forgave and moved on. Hard as this was, we were learning more about our communication styles and problem solving skills, and felt freedom to express our opinions without reproach. It was a good first test for us.

In the later part of January, we went on the singles ski retreat in Virginia at the same location I'd attended a year earlier. The weekend was a combination of fellowship, listening to guest speakers, hiking, and skiing. This was our first trip together, and we had a great time along with our friends. Halfway home we stopped at a restaurant. Before we were got out of Jon's truck he told me he loved me. He said he wasn't sure if he was in love with me, but he felt he was starting to fall in love. I wasn't sure if I loved him yet, and told him I wasn't ready to say those words. Although we'd discussed marriage and children, I was too scared to say I was in love. Being a tenacious lover, once I told him I loved him, and committed my heart, there was no turning back without a lot of pain. Poor guy, I know that's not what he wanted to hear but I had to be honest.

Three weeks later it was Valentine's Day, and Jon surprised me with a vase of 18 pink, red and white roses delivered to our restaurant dinner table. They were gorgeous! All eyes were on us, and people were smiling, when Jon handed me a poem he'd written for the occasion. He told me the twins helped him devise the plan of surprising me with roses at dinner. I was so touched, and started to realize that a family was opening up their heart to me, not just Jon. We had a fabulous meal and slow danced for the first time to the music the live band was playing. A close friend of ours was there with her boyfriend too, and took our picture as we held hands at dinner. As I walked out of the restaurant, carrying that vase of long stem roses, I felt like a prom queen! It was such a romantic gesture of his love for me.

When Jon took me back to my apartment he asked if we could have our first passionate kiss on Valentine's Day, and so we did. I knew I was fighting back my feelings of love for Jon out of fear. In my past relationships, things seemed to go downhill once the guy knew I loved him. I was afraid things would change between us, and not in a good way, if I told him I loved him. In my angst, I decided to hold back a little while longer. Neither of us said, "I love you" after that wonderful Valentine's Day meal and kiss. The night was magical enough without those words. Jon hadn't said them to me again since the first time he spoke them after the ski retreat.

Over the next few days I cried out loud to God over how insecure I was. I pleaded with Jesus to reveal if there was any reason I should not tell Jon I loved him, or keep moving forward. Three days later I had no cautionary warnings from heaven, and knew I was falling in love. So I took the leap of faith, and told Jon I loved him. It was a powerful and happy moment for both of us; one that we kept private. Everyone knew we really liked each, but we weren't ready to announce to the world yet that we were in love. He hadn't met my family, so we made flight arrangements to go to Syracuse the end of March. He really wanted to meet everyone, and I was excited for them to see us together. It had been many years since I brought a guy home for my family to meet.

Now that we were kissing the temptation for sexual intimacy increased, so we didn't stay alone together long enough to get ourselves into trouble. It also helped me to continue meeting with my mentor. Her counsel was so wise. She said by practicing self-control in our physical relationship, God was teaching us self-restraint that could benefit us in other areas. If we got married, we were giving ourselves a greater chance of success by denying our passions now. My mentor believed when we sacrifice instant gratification; controlling our longings in one area, we draw from the knowledge gained from that experience; using it during other circumstances. We'd begin to see how God helped us accomplish this task. This would grow our faith in Him for strength to control our desires and make for a balanced life physically, emotionally, and spiritually.

Jon and I were witnessing first-hand how practicing self-control and abstinence increased our trust in each other too. Because we were able to resist sexual temptation when we were together, it gave us greater confidence that we would resist the temptation of others when we were apart—such as traveling for business. This was very important to both of us since we had been deceived in the past by former lovers, and never wanted to experience that kind of betrayal again.

Because we were talking, more than we were kissing, we often paused to look at our relationship from a practical versus romantic view. Jon used the example that marriage is similar to two companies merging. You have to look at how your partner runs their business. Are they a person of integrity whose actions line up with their words, or is there a discrepancy between what they say and how they live? He raised some valuable points which led us to review a mission statement Jon had created years ago after following the advice of a church counselor. Jon didn't want to take away from the romance and spontaneity of our courtship, but professed when you're considering marrying someone you have to evaluate things logically; not just emotionally. He believed God gave us our brains to use along with our hearts when making decisions. If I was willing, Jon wanted us to write our own mission statement.

The purpose of creating a mission statement was to see if our vision of marriage was the same and if not, what did we want to re-write together? If it was a contrasting vision, or neither one of us was living our life as a reflection of our mission statement, then that would indicate a problem that needed to be addressed before marriage. We were well aware going forward would require a leap of faith no matter what, but we didn't want to proceed naively without some sound reasons, and God's blessing on our union. A decision to get married shouldn't be based on the hope that the Lord will fix grievances between us when He might be sending us signs in advance not to marry each other in the first place. Initially, I was caught off guard by this mission statement, but slowly it became another reason I was attracted to Jon. It showed me that he was just as committed as I was to having a healthy and thriving marriage, and that was very exciting to me!

As we flew to Syracuse in late-March, Jon said he would never propose to me without asking my father's permission first. I replied, "You're not going to ask him something so important the first time you meet him are you?" He assured me he wouldn't. Being a father of three daughters himself, he wanted to show my father respect by asking for my hand before we got engaged. I couldn't believe how considerate he was, and it made me love him even more. After meeting Jon, my normally cautious family gave their wholehearted approval to our dating, and thought we were a great match for each other. Jon fit right in with everyone; making the weekend a great success. Next it was my turn to meet Jon's oldest daughter. She came to Raleigh for a visit a few days later. It was fun watching her interact with her father and sisters, and she was very relaxed around me. What a blessing to feel so comfortable around each other's families.

As we moved into April, I found myself thinking about how much my life had changed in a year. It was hard to believe on April 19th I'd mark the one-year anniversary of my surgery by celebrating how terrific I felt. My energy was back and even though I still had some tenderness in my abdomen around my scar, I felt incredible physically and emotionally. Many times I wept; overcome with joy and gratitude for all the ways God had blessed me. What a miraculous year it had been for me! *How could life possibly get any better than this?*

Chapter 22
From Hospital Gown to Wedding Gown

"I will repay you for the years the locust have eaten" (Joel 2:25 NIV).

S pringtime in Raleigh is glorious and April, 2002 was no exception. Never before had I lived in a place with so many flowering trees and bushes. As Jon and I continued our ritual of early evening walks, I felt such a peace being around him. I was completely content with the pace of our relationship, and in no rush to accelerate it. The way things were going, it looked like we might be engaged by December, and planning a wedding for the spring or summer of 2003. Even though there was no guarantee we would be engaged by the end of the year, our honest and open pursuit of the subject of a life together left me feeling very comfortable. Our love for each other was growing stronger with each passing day.

One balmy evening as we walked around the lake savoring the fragrant air, Jon suggested we plan a day-trip to tour a bed and breakfast an hour-and-a-half south of Raleigh. He thought it might be a nice setting for a wedding reception. Reluctantly I replied, "Aren't we getting a bit ahead of ourselves? I know we've discussed marriage, but we're not engaged yet." Jon persisted in his attempt to persuade me, "I don't want to spoil the surprise, but I think you know I'm seriously considering proposing sometime this year. Because reception locations often have to be reserved a year in advance, why not start looking now to see what we like?" *Touché--he got me there!* Although tentative, I agreed to go exploring with him.

Saturday morning April 13th was sunny and warm when Jon picked me up at 10 AM. Feeling very emotional, I told Jon I was overwhelmed by all that God had done in my life. He'd healed me from the inside out; every part of me had been touched so profoundly by God's grace and love. As if the gift of good health wasn't enough, God went even further by bringing Jon into my life. For that, I was immeasurably grateful. Jon listened attentively and smiled as I cried. While I was reliving the memories of where I was in life physically, emotionally, and spiritually a year ago compared to now, I couldn't understand why I was unable to stop crying! *What was wrong with me?* It was rather embarrassing, but at least this time they were tears of joy.

I composed myself by the time we reached the bed and breakfast, and introduced ourselves to the wedding planner. We explained we weren't engaged yet, but gathering facts on the cost and availability of this location in case we chose it for our reception. She reviewed the amenities, and after about 30 minutes, Jon said we should probably walk around the grounds ourselves. She was very accommodating, and understood we weren't ready to make any commitments that day. We thanked her for the information, saying we'd stop back inside the Inn before we left for Raleigh.

Walking by a pond, we spotted a pretty stone bench under a white dogwood tree in bloom. Jon asked me to sit down for a minute as he sat beside me. He looked away from me, focusing straight ahead on the pond, while he asked me questions. I thought his behavior was odd; he seemed nervous. He asked if I could picture myself getting married in a field near the pond. *Not really.* I told him I wasn't sure about having an outdoor wedding ceremony. I envisioned an indoor/outdoor reception where people could casually move around visiting one another, but I preferred a church ceremony.

As Jon continued his questioning, he took my right hand into his left; playing with the ruby birthstone ring I wore. While never gazing off the pond, he asked me if I would marry him. I thought he was kidding because he didn't say anything else. I wasn't sure I heard him correctly. I think I was in shock! Then I looked down at my right hand and saw he'd slipped a three-stone diamond ring on my finger, and was pushing it on top of the ruby ring! I gasped, "Oh, you're not kidding, but look, you're putting it on the wrong hand!" Jon laughed and said, "I'm so nervous!" Then he put the ring on my left hand and I said, "Yes!" We were both crying as I looked at my wrist watch; noting it was 12:10 PM when we were officially engaged.

Facing each other; smiling as I said, "Well, I guess this

155

means you're not going to ask my father's permission." All choked up Jon replied, "Your dad, mom and siblings already know. I called them two nights ago to ask their permission when you were eating dinner with your girl-friends. I hope I didn't spoil your surprise, honey." *No way did he spoil my surprise! This was perfect!* In fact, he was a man of his word. Just as he'd promised, he'd asked for permission. Snuggled face-to-face on that stone bench laughing, crying and praying together, it was hard to fathom this April, unlike the last, I'd be donning a wedding gown; not a hospital gown. Jon admitted proposing here hoping this was our reception choice. He imagined showing guests where he'd asked me. *Great idea!*

Always prepared for a photo opportunity, I'd brought my camera anticipating we'd take shots of the Inn as a record of a possible reception site. How convenient! Walking back to the Inn, we asked the wedding planner if she'd take our photo where we got engaged. She happily agreed. Then Jon asked her what time of year made for a pretty outdoor reception. She suggested September. We had our choice of September 7th or 28th. *Did he really want to get married in five months?* This was happening so fast it seemed surreal. When I woke up this morning I never imagined I'd become a fiancé who'd be selecting her wedding date and location today! Jon joked about picking September 28th because that's his birthday, but he chose September 7th. The wedding planner penciled us in as we scheduled a time to reconvene with our security deposit, and to discuss all the details. A bride with no plan I wouldn't remain for long!

We stopped for lunch in the Village of Pinehurst not far from the bed and breakfast. Thinking we might spend our wedding night in Pinehurst, we walked around the quaint village before heading back to Raleigh. We had plans to meet some friends at a Durham Bulls baseball game that night, and didn't want to be late. While driving home, Jon confessed he'd spoken with several energy traders yesterday from various utility companies that he worked with. He told them he planned to propose to me today, and said half the country was probably talking about us. He was excited to go into work tomorrow and let them all know I'd said yes. He's definitely not able to keep a secret when he's got good news to share, and I love him for that!

Greeting our friends with the surprise news of our engagement, they shared in the joy of our announcement. No one really watched the baseball game--we were too busy talking about the day's events! Later that night, I called my family; asking some to be in our wedding party. Excitement filled the air as I promised more details later, urging them to save the date of September 7th. Sunday found me calling beloved friends we'd chosen as greeters, ushers, and Scripture readers. All were thrilled and couldn't wait to celebrate with us! Taking a break, I met Jon in his downtown office. Proudly, he informed me the lines were buzzing with the news of our engagement traveling the eastern states among the power marketers. *He was right-- half the country was talking about us!* By Monday, I'd emailed everyone we planned to invite to the wedding; releasing the floodgates allowing happy responses to pour into my inbox. What a precious time this was as the Lord put a continuous song of praise in my heart!

A short time later, I told Jon although I was 43 sometimes I felt 23, only much more grounded and wiser than I was before. It was as if my life had been renewed and restored, and I was being paid back for all those lost years. Knowing I wasn't deserving of the favor God had bestowed on me made me even more amazed at how He answered my petitions. God's response was better than anything I could have imagined! Even though I was a middle-aged bride, I felt youthful and so vibrant. What an enchanting season in my life; this was at last my happy storybook ending. My nieces and nephews affectionately began referring to me as "Aunt Cinderella", which only added to the magic of it all. But just to keep us humble, and bring us back to reality from this dreamlike state, God was about to introduce some new and challenging experiences into our lives.

Chapter 23
Trusting During Trials

"Test me in this, says the Lord Almighty, and see if I will not throw open the floodgates of heaven and pour out so much blessing that you will not have room enough for it" (Malachi 3:10 NIV).

May 1st we flew with the twins to Montana to visit Jon's sister and brother-in-law. They'd moved there from North Dakota, where Jon was born. With their parents deceased, Jon's sister was his closest living relative. His family was very welcoming, and I enjoyed seeing Jon and the twins visit with people they hadn't seen in awhile. We stayed a few nights in Deer Lodge then headed to Glacier National Park where we'd rented a three-bedroom house. The twins sanctioned us sharing a bedroom if we wanted to, but Jon refreshed their memories. Sleeping together was not something we'd do until we were married.

It was interesting observing how people reacted when told we weren't living or sleeping together until marriage. In most circles purity and holiness aren't discussed. People assume if you're in love you should act on those feelings rather than practice restraint. Some couldn't understand why Jon and I choose celibacy, while secretly many women shared with me they wished they'd waited until their wedding night. There was always a twinge of regret in their voice. Having been in their situation years earlier, I understood their remorse. Premarital sex only served to make me feel more insecure, and shameful about our relationship. Now that I had been given a chance to save sex for marriage, I wasn't going to let it slip away.

Our obedience to dating God's way was a demonstration of our love for Him. We trusted His way of doing things was better than ours. As followers of Christ we're called to be imitators of Him, realizing we represent a holy and pure God. We are not alone in this mission; the Father gives us a Helper. The Holy Spirit helps us stay committed. "Greater is He who is in me than he who is in the world" (1 John 4:4 NIV). It was God-power, not our will power that would enable us to remain celibate until our wedding. In my heart I knew we weren't sacrificing sex before marriage in order to get God to give us something. God blesses all of us whether we deserve it or not. Staying sexually pure not only increased my love for Jon, but my passion and respect for him too. It was one of the many ways God blessed us throughout our courtship.

Later in May, I had my annual doctor visit while Jon was exploring the possibility of additional children. We went to our appointments separately; agreeing to report back about our conception chances. During the ultrasound exam, the doctor circled a few fibroids. Hearing the word "fibroids" terrified me. Thankfully, they were few in number and dime-size in circumference; nothing to worry about. He turned the screen towards me revealing I was about to ovulate, "Look, you could go home and get pregnant tonight!" How encouraging to hear those words, especially at age 43, but I informed him we were waiting until our wedding night. I left there feeling optimistic motherhood was possible, but not sure it was realistic. Because of my medical history, I'd be a high-risk pregnancy, and was guaranteed a cesarean birth. The thought of being operated on again frightened me. Still, I was willing to endure it if Jon wanted children with me.

Jon's news was not as promising. His medical procedure to father a child cost $12,000. This wasn't covered by insurance, and we didn't have the funds. There was a slim possibility we could conceive without Jon undergoing surgery, but it would be a miracle. We discussed the immense cost of raising a child, and our current financial commitments with Jon's girls in college. Well aware that God could provide for us if He brought another child into our lives, given our obligations it didn't appear to be wise to add another child to the family without His blessing. *How could I ask Jon's girls to sacrifice their college education so I could pursue my dream of motherhood? That didn't seem fair to them.* I believed our first priority was to the children that already existed in our lives, and yet I didn't want to close the door entirely without praying one last time. There was no complete unity between us with Jon still being unsure about adding to the family, and me ready to move in that direction. Without mutual consent there was no moving forward; so I asked the Lord to change one of our hearts to align with His will for our lives.

Confronted again with this torturous desire to procreate refusing to die, doubt entered in. *Lord, I confess this doesn't seem fair. Why is Jon getting all he prayed for and I'm not? Whose heart has to be changed?* Far from infallible, I was tempted to manipulate Jon's generous spirit into appeasing me realizing God knows the future; not me. *Did I lack the faith to trust Him; would my selfish ambitions override Christ's plans?* Wrestling with God in my soul, I felt His gentle urging to release the dream; offering no explanation, only His peace. Wanting a baby wasn't a wrong desire, but it couldn't be the source of my happiness as I'd made it for so long. Faith isn't the absence of doubt. It's simply moving forward; holding God's hand without complete understanding. If I wanted to feel lasting pleasure, not temporary happiness based on life's experiences, only Jesus could supply that. "You've made known to me the path of life; you will fill me with joy in your presence, with eternal pleasures at your right hand" (Psalm 16:11 NIV).

After much prayer, it was my heart God changed as I told Jon I no longer wanted to pursue motherhood. Knowing what this choice cost me, Jon pressed me further; looking for assurance I wasn't resentful. While saddened by the death of my dream, I held no grudges towards Jon, or God. Having shed rivers of tears over this topic, I knew with certainty Jesus was asking me to relinquish it. Although I lacked complete clarity as to why, God owed me no explanation. Healing isn't a linear process; in time Jesus would turn my grief into dancing. Even as I shared with Jon my choice to remain childless, I experienced joy in obedience. If God wanted me to get pregnant, He could perform a miracle. The choice was His alone. I would no longer attempt to make it happen myself.

June brought two major tests simultaneously. First, we had to forfeit our wedding location. The Inn was under renovation, and management couldn't guarantee completion by September 7th. With 10 weeks to go, we had to start over. Initially, panic set in upon hearing our wedding had to be rearranged. I knew the date was firm. Many of our guests had purchased airline tickets, and the photographer and Disc Jockey we'd reserved were not available on other September dates. As anxiety built inside of me, I paused to pray. Then with a calm voice I said to God, "You must have something really special in mind for our wedding since you allowed this to happen." Now I was excited! Whatever He had planned, I knew it would surpass my grandest expectations, and I couldn't wait to see what it was.

Jon and I rendezvoused that night; dividing up the list of tasks. We contacted the singles pastor who was marrying us, and learned our church was available for September 7th. This was good news and a better choice for us versus our original location more than an hour's drive away. After all, Providence Baptist Church was where Jon first noticed me. Visiting a friend who was helping me design my handmade invitations, we decided to browse reception web sites. One in particular caught my attention. It was the Matthews House, a beautifully restored white pillar Grecian-style home with a large private yard. When Jon viewed their website he liked it too; so I made an appointment for a tour the following week. Other places we called were already booked or were too expensive. With time running out, a decision had to be made soon.

The second test came a few days before our Matthews House tour. I received word that my recruiting contract position was ending mid-July due to an economic slow down.

What a blessing to have had this contract for 10 months, but it was bad timing losing my job with a wedding on the horizon. Concerned about our finances; the vision for our wedding began to change in Jon's mind. In his fearful state, he presented me with two options he'd devised. One involved breaking my apartment lease and moving into the condo with Jon and the twins. One of us would sleep on the couch until we got married. The girls were fine with it, but I wasn't comfortable.

The second option was to cancel everything and substitute it with a small private ceremony, minus a reception, before September. That wouldn't work, in my opinion. From the moment we announced our engagement people insisted on a big reception, saying they'd waited years for this celebration. I wanted that too. Deep in my heart, I knew if we succumbed to fear and eloped, our wedding day wouldn't be very special. Tearfully, I told Jon that while I understood his concerns about finances, and appreciated his suggestions, I believed this wedding was bigger than us. There was a reason we'd faced so much opposition. It wasn't God trying to prevent us from getting married. Rather something good was going to happen that day, besides our union. I thought the Matthews House was worth investigating to evaluate the cost. Jon sympathetically agreed, so the appointment was kept.

As we toured the Matthews House, later that week, we instantly loved what we saw. What a feast for the eyes! All the furnishings and accompaniments in the two-story house were so lavish we wouldn't need to spend additional money on decorations. To our delight, the property manager said the only weekend available was September 6-8th. All others were booked until spring 2003. *Incredible!* We'd have access to the house all day Friday through noon on Sunday if we paid to stay in their honeymoon suite. In addition, we were granted permission to provide a continental brunch on September 8th for our guests. Saddened by our recent trials, she generously gave us a discount. Our wish had come true! It was a beautiful facility close to the church, hotels, airport, and the cost was less than we'd budgeted. Another gift from God beyond our expectations!

We announced our new reception location during our engagement party on June 29th at my matron-of-honor's home. Our friends couldn't believe we'd planned an entirely different wedding within a week. The leasing manager of my apartment complex was non-negotiable on breaking my lease, or giving me a discount on my rent, so it made no sense to move prior to September. While we could have saved money by eloping, we decided to believe God would provide for us. He'd already given us a less expensive wedding package, so we'd be okay. Despite the recent turmoil things were falling into place, and we were excited about our upcoming day.

The summer was busy with another friend's wedding in Raleigh, entertaining family visitors in July, and the twins moving to California to finish their college studies; living with their mother and sister. We were no longer worried about expenses; we'd stayed within the bounds of our budget. Our entire wedding was prepaid with cash, so there were no loans or credit card bills to consume us. We'd always promised we wouldn't create debt for ourselves around this day. Unique as it was, we saw no value in overspending on something so soon forgotten. Our guests would remember the fun they had, and how happy we were, but they won't recall many of the details of the day.

It felt good to have learned how to plan a very beautiful and distinctive wedding day without breaking the bank, or creating a lot of tension between us!

August afforded us a trip to see my good friends in Buffalo whose wedding I'd been in four years earlier. We visited Niagara Falls with them before attending another close friend's wedding in the Buffalo area. Two days later, Jon and I drove to Syracuse where my family did a fabulous job hosting my bridal shower on August 4th. Filled with so much hope and joy about my future with Jon, it was the happiest time of my life. As the RSVPs came in, the list included people who haven't seen or spoken to each other in years. Still nursing old wounds, some of these guests revealed their fears around seeing people they'd been at odds with. Knowing their hesitancy was due to an unforgiving heart, I prayed God would take care of everything. It would take His intervention for these individuals to reconcile with each other, so I asked for a miracle. My greatest wish was for a peaceful wedding, and that healing would take place in the lives of those who needed it. Beseeching the Holy Spirit to work in a mighty way that September weekend, I prayed the name of Jesus would be magnified. Naturally, the focus would be on Jon and me as the bride and groom, but I wanted God to get the glory for the whole event.

From time to time, there were many things I fussed over. *Would the food taste good; did I order enough? Are the flowers the best choice? Was there someone I forgot to include? Will I look good in my gown? How do I coordinate the timing of everything? Are the honeymoon details confirmed? What about the colors I selected?* My hope was my bridesmaids wouldn't be cringing years later as they looked at photos and asked themselves, "Why did Mary make me wear that?!" Some nights I'd toss and turn wondering if I'd forgotten something. Picturing the event, I prayed for good weather and a day of perfect harmony. I asked Jesus to give me rest during this hectic season, and to guard against attempts to steal my peace. While much of my attention was devoted to the wedding, I never lost sight of the fact that this was only the start of my life with Jon; preparing for our marriage took precedence. The closer we got to the date, the more my excitement grew. Beyond our vows, something really special was going to happen that day. Knowing how much I love surprises, the Lord was about to usher in a big one as I'd witness answered prayers, and another "Red Sea" miracle.

Chapter 24
A Joyful Celebration

"See! The winter is past; the rains are over and gone. Flowers appear on the earth; the season of singing has come, the cooing of doves is heard in our land. The fig tree forms its early fruit; the blossoming vines spread their fragrance. Arise, come, my darling; my beautiful one, come with me" (Solomon Song of Songs 2:11-13 NIV).

As September approached, we pushed aside the busyness of wedding planning to further discuss our vision of married life. We revealed our pet peeves, hoping not to commit many of them once we were living under the same roof, and defined some of our roles and responsibilities. Nothing was regimented, and our attitudes were flexible, but it was nice to have some idea of the expectation. We talked about what our sex life might be like, and while details were limited, it helped to establish some guidelines knowing we'd grow in this area as time passed. Jon insisted if we had unresolved conflict in our marriage we'd seek church counseling immediately, rather than let animosity fester. Throughout our courtship his reactions and willingness to talk with me, seek advice from godly people, and solve problems quickly was all the assurance I could ask for. Jesus was with us too. "For the eyes of the Lord range throughout the earth to strengthen those whose hearts are fully committed to Him" (2 Chronicles 16:9 NIV). Trusting Jon was God's choice for me, I didn't need to live with him outside of marriage to find out if it was right. God already confirmed His blessing on our union; He could be counted on to keep His promise to help us. Our prenuptial agreement was with Him, not with lawyers, as we trusted all we were bringing into our marriage God was watching over. It was all His anyway; we were only guardians of what He'd provided.

Festivities were in full swing as guests began arriving in Raleigh on Wednesday, September 4th. The forecast called for 86 degrees and low humidity throughout the next five days. What a welcomed treat after such a hot summer! Our Friday night rehearsal dinner party was held at the pool of my apartment complex. Not an unkind word was spoken between anyone, and conversations were flowing smoothly right from the start. What a great way to begin our weekend of celebration! I spent my last night as a single woman with my spiritual big sister as my apartment guest. We sat in my living room talking, laughing, crying, and praying until 11 PM. It was a sweet time as we looked back on all that God had done in our lives. She prayed a blessing upon Jon and me, and I fell asleep confident Jesus was in our midst.

At 7:00 AM Saturday, September 7th before my girlfriend

awoke I hurried down to Lake Lynn to spend time with God. Standing on a bridge, below my apartment building, my heart leapt with joy as I humbly said, "I'm the bride. It's finally my turn!" Soon my apartment would be bustling with activity as bridesmaids primped themselves (and me) before heading to church. This was the last moment I'd have alone with God. After 10 minutes, I ran back to my apartment and began preparing for my wedding day. By 10:00 AM my kitchen table was transformed into an assembly line of girls getting their hair and nails done. I was snapping photos until my hairdresser sister sat me down. What team work! Everyone was helping someone; filling the room with happy chatter. As she tossed my curls on top of my head; adorning them with rhinestones, my sister cried saying, "Mary, you look so beautiful!" Determined not to cry and show the camera my eyes puffy red eyes today, I laughed in reply, "I can't look that good without make up!" God had given me grace and favor on my wedding day, making me into a pretty joy-filled bride. The treasured season of anticipation that came with engagement was over, and the day I'd dreamed of was here at last!

We left for the bride's room at church around 12:30 PM where we'd change into our gowns. As I put my key in the lock, I took one last look, knowing the next time I walked through this door I'd be a married woman. Whispering a thank you to Jesus, I quietly shut the door on my current dwelling place, as I looked forward to my new one. God changed my life on that warm October night in 2001 when I met Jon walking around Lake Lynn. Now it was time to walk down the isle into his life forever.

Jon's daughters arrived from California and came rushing into the bride's room to see me. They delivered a note that

Jon had written to me about how excited he was to marry me. The girls jumped right in helping inflate helium balloons that the guests would release outdoors after our ceremony. One of my sister-in-laws suggested attaching a Scripture to the tether, so I chose John 10:10 (NIV): "The thief comes only to steal and kill and destroy: I have come that they may have life, and have it to the full." What a day to share the abundant life we have as believers in Jesus Christ as our Messiah!

Surrounded by our wedding party I was overcome with emotion as I gazed upon these special people: my matron-of-honor who along with her husband helped me relocate to Raleigh, my sisters and nieces wearing sage green bridesmaids dresses with pale pink accents, my nephews as double ring bearers and another one as a groomsman in black and sage attire, friends of ours as ushers and groomsmen, my girlfriends from New Hampshire and Raleigh that greeted our guests arriving at church, my Buffalo friend beside her husband who read Psalm 145 along with my Atlanta spiritual big sister reading Romans 12:9-13. Having so many people I loved in one place was truly an incredible feeling.

Our wedding day fell on a high holiday for my Jewish friends who initially debated between attending Temple services or our ceremony. It was Rosh Hashanah, and I was thrilled they'd chosen to celebrate with us; telling them not to worry, God was there too! Somehow it seemed appropriate for Jon and me to be married on the Jewish Civil New Year. It's referred to as the Feast of Trumpets in Leviticus 23:23-25 (NIV), "The Lord said to Moses, Say to the Israelites: On the first day of the seventh month you are to have a day of rest, a sacred assembly commemorated

with trumpet blasts. Do no regular work, but present an offering made to the Lord by fire." Rosh Hashanah is a time
of rejoicing and of new beginnings just as my wedding day
was! Even my wedding march, "Trumpet Tune", matched
the occasion!

At 2:00 PM, in my strapless dazzling white gown, I walked
down the isle on the arm of my father who was telling me
jokes to keep me relaxed. I wasn't fearful of my decision to
marry Jon, just experiencing some stage fright as all eyes in
the church were on me! Those few minutes strolling with
my dad were bittersweet. I knew he was happy for me, but I
could feel his heart aching too. It's not always easy to let
go of someone you've held onto for so long, but he and my
mother had prepared me well for this day. I wondered how
often he'd imagined this day when I was growing up. Fa-
thers and daughters don't get many spotlight moments it
seems, but this one was ours together, and I wanted to ab-
sorb every second before it was gone.

Facing Jon to take our vows so many thoughts ran through
my mind. My knees were shaking a little as I silently
thought, *"This man is marrying me and we haven't seen
each other naked!"* I felt so loved and treasured by Jon
who was taking me as his wife based on things that would
last longer than our physical bodies would. The joy in waiting until my wedding day was that I felt no shame before
the Lord, or the congregation. I also felt more secure in
Jon's love and commitment to our marriage. We had persevered together in the battle for purity, and in the process
we'd fallen deeply in love with each other's character and
interior beauty. God doesn't give us blessings because we
are righteous and behave well enough to earn His favor, but
He blesses us out of His love and goodness. The blessing

Jon and I received that day was in knowing we'd been obedient, letting Jesus shape our hearts and prepare us for marriage.

As I stood there and made a covenant with Jon and God, I knew Jesus was eager to help us. "The Lord will keep you from all harm—He will watch over your life; the Lord will watch over your coming and going both now and forevermore Psalm 121:7-8" NIV). When the ceremony ended, I left the altar a happy wife beside my handsome husband, while the organist played "Climb Every Mountain" from the Sound of Music. We passed through an arch of bubbles my nephews were blowing outside the church, where our guests let their white balloons soar towards the bright blue heaven. As we were escorted away in a friend's BMW to have photos taken at Lake Lynn, we felt like royalty.

The Matthews House perfectly matched the indoor-outdoor reception we'd envisioned. The bartender served drinks on the backyard wrap-around porch, while guests danced under a canopy of white lights on trees. They mingled around the grounds after filling their plates inside, as children laughed and played in the grass. Throughout the day, we heard many wonderful compliments; pleasing us to know people enjoyed this pretty house setting. After a grand celebration, we began our good-byes around 9:30 PM.

Many of our out-of-town guests would join us for brunch in the morning, except for my father. He was driving home to Syracuse early; the others were flying out Sunday afternoon. Thanking my dad, as I kissed him goodbye, I handed him goodies I'd baked for his trip. I wish we'd talked longer, but there were other guests clamoring for my attention. Exchanging hugs with friends, their lovely words moved me to tears. How wonderful to shed tears prompted by joy!

Jon and I were nervous as any bride and groom would be on their wedding night, but that made the moment even more magical and special for us. The following morning we welcomed our guests back to the Matthews House at 10:00 AM. September 7th brought people together who by September 8th had forgiven each other; releasing the pain they'd tightly embraced for years. When they tearfully told us the conversations they'd had the day before at our wedding reception, and how they were led to reconciliation, we were bursting at the seams with gratitude over all that Jesus had done. The day was a new beginning not just for Jon and me, but for so many people we loved too. Their "Red Sea" of bitterness had been parted at last. What a great wedding present we'd been given!

Chapter 25
Looking Back While Moving Forward

"The Spirit of the sovereign Lord is on me, because the
Lord has anointed me to preach good news to the poor.
He has sent me to bind up the brokenhearted, to proclaim freedom for the captives and release from darkness for the prisoners, to proclaim the year of the
Lord's favor and the day of vengeance of our God, to
comfort all who mourn" (Isaiah 61:1-2 NIV).

The healing that occurred at our wedding propelled
many of our guests to a higher level of love and acceptance, and strife no longer reigned in the lives of those
whose hearts were previously unforgiving. While the joy
remained, our wedding festivities were short-lived. Within
eight weeks we went from the mountain top of celebrating
in September to the valley of mourning in November, with
the unexpected death of my father from a ruptured aortic
aneurysm. Reaction upon hearing Jon's strained voice tell-

ing me my father had died confirmed once more I was not alone. My response was not what I'd call normal, at least not for me. I'm convinced I could only utter these words because God's Holy Spirit was comforting my soul. I wept in disbelief and yet I smiled as I said, "Praise God. The Lord is so good to our family, Jon. He didn't let Dad suffer but took him quickly. I'm so thankful for that."

I sobbed the entire 11-hour drive with Jon from Raleigh to Syracuse for my father's funeral. Forevermore my wedding day would be the last time I'd see Dad. Suddenly it was clear to Jon and me that if we'd eloped we'd never have witnessed Christ's restorative power working in the hearts of our wedding guests who were now assembled at Dad's funeral. Several proclaimed they would not have attended the funeral if the wedding hadn't brought them together where reconciliation occurred. In retrospect, our wedding day really wasn't about us. It was about our glorious God using the event to reveal His love and demonstrate He's always at work in our lives.

The last phone conversation with my father, shortly before his death, was filled with laughter and no regrets. It was one of the most interesting exchanges I'd ever had with him. A few minutes into the call my mind began wandering. Taking the moment for granted, I was fidgeting around the condo when I heard this voice whisper to me, *"Mary, Mary pay very close attention."* Immediately I stopped pacing and hung on every word my father spoke. I had no idea then it was the last time we'd ever speak. But God knew, and I believe it was His voice that prompted me to listen to my dad that evening.

Before we hung up, Dad asked me what a Baptist baptismal

ceremony was like. I told him babies were not baptized as infants like the church he and Mom raised me in. Instead, they're dedicated to the Lord with the belief they'll be baptized with water one day when they've confessed their sins, and accepted in their heart that Jesus is their Messiah. Their baptism is an outward sign to everyone of their inward commitment to God, and that they've been saved and born again spiritually by His grace. My father replied he thought that was really nice, and I sensed the Holy Spirit had directed our conversation. To this day, I am so thankful for these memories and for God's hand on our family over the years.

Upon completion of this book, Jon and I are happily celebrating our sixth wedding anniversary. The years have tested our young marriage with three job losses for me, acclimating into Jon's pre-existing family, and the pain associated with struggles of loved ones we desperately want to help. Through it all, we've grown closer as a couple; more dependent on the Creator and Sustainer of everything, Jesus. With God on our side, it's Jon and Mary working in tandem battling against life's storms, not Jon and Mary fighting against each other. We're continually learning that God's blessings aren't always found in good times and happy things. Trials and hardship are what He uses to bring us to a higher level of understanding of His unsurpassed power and mercy. We welcome His instruction regardless of the circumstances.

Whenever we are stricken with the "Moses Syndrome" (my term for feeling inadequate to handle the situation we're in), we are quickly reminded that God specializes in miracles and impossibilities. Like trusting the harness of a zip-line to support us as we leap off our safe platform, so it is with God as we put our faith in His protection during times of uncertainty. Whatever He's allowed into our lives is preparation for something greater, even if it's something difficult. We're guaranteed the blessing of contentment if we stand firm on His Word, and the promise of His provision. The lessons we learned while dating of practicing self-control physically and financially, in addition to crafting a mission statement, have translated into many marital benefits. We often review our goals; smiling over the progress we've made, adjusting as necessary. While finding contentment in all of life's adversities remains a life-long challenge we'll never fully master, we marvel in gratitude at the help God provides.

When I was single, my dream was to have a peaceful and loving home with my husband. The Lord has been very gracious to us; our house is a sanctuary for us as well as our guests. The material gifts Christ has given us are not only for our pleasure, but to share with others in our lives. In 2004 we sold our condo and moved into a new house that provided extra space for entertaining, and temporary shelter for family members needing a retreat in times of crisis. During our house-hunting excursions, Jon and I prayed for God to show us where He wanted us to be. We didn't want to buy anything above our means. After a year of searching, God revealed the perfect home for us. We've enjoyed practicing the gift of hospitality, and sharing this blessing with loved ones.

Reflecting back on how I prayed for my future husband and the life I envisioned, God answered all these prayers, but some in a different way. I never had the miracle baby I hoped for, even though at age 47 another ultrasound revealed I was still ovulating. Fashioned as a passionate nurturer, not a robotic zombie void of emotions, there are fleeting moments of sadness over the realization no one calls me mom. But the pain quickly fades, and I know my life is as it's supposed to be. My heart is forever rejoicing over the gift of good health; I'm no longer plagued by any problems associated with uterine fibroids. After a two-year post-surgery sabbatical from chocolate and caffeine (thought impossible to eliminate by some!), I enjoy all food and drink without suffering any adverse effects.

Having handed my scepter to the King of my life, Jesus continues to shape me into the wife and stepmother He desires me to be. Although Jon and I are not perfect people, we are perfectly suited because God joined us. Not a day goes by when we don't speak a gentle word; keeping our promise to be good to each other. Similar to our courtship, we continually practice edifying and encouraging each other. By God's grace, I have the happy home, loving marriage, and harmonious blended family I prayed for. Daily I seek to protect and nurture these blessings out of my love for my husband, and my heavenly Father who entrusted me with them.

As for my girlfriends who prayed with me for men that fateful summer of 2001, all of them were married by 2006 including my spiritual big sister in Atlanta who taught me how to pray for my husband as if I already knew him! Most of us have children in our lives either as stepmothers or natural births. Each of our stories is unique in how God chose to answer our prayers, and each brings praise to His name. We continue to stay in touch regularly; sharing in our joys and sorrows along the journey. Their friendship still keeps me accountable and encourages me in my faith walk as does my relationship with my mentor. Although she has moved out of state, we've stayed in contact over the years. I praise God for the way He spoke to me through this humble woman of faith.

When I think about all the things that have brought me happiness over the past few years, every one of them points back to God's grace in my life. While Jon brings me so much joy, my joy first began with a close relationship with Jesus who invaded my heart with His extravagant love. Jon didn't rescue me from loneliness, Jesus did. Jon's not my Savior, Jesus is. Jon completes the circle of love, but he didn't start it. Christ, in His love for me, drew me close to Him and satisfied my soul before He introduced me to Jon. I would have never attracted the quality of man Jon is without the healing power of the Holy Spirit working in my life first. Jon is one of God's greatest gifts to me. There is nothing I did to earn or deserve him. By surrendering the outcome to Jesus, I learned to find contentment in Him, and stopped striving to find a husband, or settle for anything less than God's perfect will for me. Even though Jon and I love each other very much, we cannot fill the space in our hearts that God created in each human being for His dwelling place.

In recent years I've learned that I was created for a purpose and a reason—to know God, to love God, and to bring glory to Him. He formed each of us with this in mind. "For by Him all things were created; all things in heaven and on earth, visible and invisible, whether thrones or powers or rulers or authorities; all things were created by Him and for Him" (Colossians 1:16 NIV). While my relationship with Jesus is very personal it's not to be kept private. Being a disciple of Christ means living a public life by loving others and sharing what God is doing in my circumstances, so

it will draw them to seek Jesus
serve wherever God has me in t

As this knowledge of being crea
and glorious purpose has taken
ticipating what new adventures
know everything God wants me
cific details aren't important. I w
pray and study His Word. My id
Jon's wife, it's found in being God s daughter. The Lord
has been faithful to all His promises, and by seeking first
His kingdom I've found righteousness, peace and joy in
knowing and loving Jesus. The best part is, the most wonderful day I'll ever experience on earth is nothing compared to what being in God's presence will be like in
heaven! "No eye has seen, no ear has heard, no mind con-
ceived what God has prepared for those who love Him" (1
Corinthians 2:9 NIV). Amen!

Time will tell what His next assignment for me is. Created
as a natural born cheerleader, I'm prone towards encouraging others, so I pray you were blessed by this story of
God's providence in my life. This book was not written to
guarantee anyone a spouse, but to promise you that having
a personal relationship with Jesus will change your heart
forever. Draw near to Jesus Christ, and let Him create the
desires in your surrendered heart that He has in mind for
you. The God who formed you into existence loves you,
and He wants to help you and give you hope for a fulfilling
life! Eternity begins while we're on earth. "Where will you
go when you die? Are you like I was, always striving to do
good works to earn your way into heaven?" However honorable and noble your deeds are, they cannot save your
soul. Take heart, it's not too late to change your course and

the Man who loves you more than any other! I
will confess your sins, your need for a Savior, and
your life to Jesus today. Then you will find God's
ravagant love invading your heart too!

Until we meet again, I leave you now with the words of the
Apostle Paul in Ephesians 3:16-21(NIV): "I pray that out of
His glorious riches He may strengthen you with power
through His Spirit in your inner being. So that Christ may
dwell in your hearts through faith. And I pray that you, being rooted and established in love, may have power, together with all the saints, to grasp how wide and long and
high and deep is the love of Christ, and to know this love
that surpasses knowledge—that you may be filled to the
measure of all the fullness of God. Now to Him who is able
to do immeasurably more than all we ask or imagine, according to His power that is at work within us, to Him be
glory in the church and in Christ Jesus throughout all generations, for ever and ever! Amen."

Blessings in Christ,
Mary Singer Wick

About the Author

Mary is a speaker and writer committed to using her gifts of exhortation and encouragement to draw women into a deeper relationship with Christ. She desires to see lives transformed as she passionately shares the work of God's Holy Spirit in her life, and the power that is available to all believers. Mary's zeal for God's Word, and her ability to communicate this love, has earned her the nickname of "Miss Enthusiasm" by those closest to her. Mary was born and raised in the suburbs of Syracuse, New York where she attended the State University of New York at Cortland earning her Bachelor's degree in Sociology. She spent 11years working and attending school in Boston, Massachusetts where she received her Master's degree from Boston College in Higher Education Administration. Upon graduation in 1995, Mary relocated to Raleigh, North Carolina to begin a new career in technical recruiting. She never dreamed she'd be a speaker and author of a published book, but God had other plans.

In 2002, shortly after becoming a first-time bride at the age of 44, Mary sensed the Lord asking her to share her story of hope with other women. Over the next five years she wrestled with God's call on her life; finally stepping forth in obedience in 2008 when she began writing *My Heart's Desire: A Journey Toward Finding Extravagant Love.* Mary and her husband Jon live in Raleigh, North Carolina. They are members of Providence Baptist Church where Mary serves in the women's mentoring program. She operates her speaking ministry under the name of Extravagant Life, LLC.

For more information please visit www.extravagantlife.net.

Breinigsville, PA USA
01 February 2010
231753BV00001B/71/P